My name is:

_____

Which means:

_____
_____
_____

EVE

THE STORY OF EVE

Once upon a time, everything we know didn't exist. There were no birds singing songs, trees swaying in the breeze, or clouds drifting in the sky. Then God decided to create.

So He spoke. With just the command of His voice, the heavens and the earth were formed. He separated the land from the water, and watched as the flowers, trees, and grass grew. The sun burst onto the scene, and after, He created the fish to swim, horses to gallop, and eagles to soar.

And after all of that creating, He decided to make human beings, male and female. God lowered His hands to the ground and formed a mound of dust, then breathed life into it. Up popped Adam, the very first man. He led Adam to an area of Earth that was especially beautiful, and there He planted the first garden. He called it Eden and told Adam that it was his job to watch over and tend to it.

Adam could eat any of the fruit and vegetables that grew there, except for the fruit that grew on one tree in the very middle. God told Adam that the tree was special, because in it was the knowledge of good and evil. Adam was not to eat of that tree, or else he would certainly die.

God watched Adam frolic through the garden and thought, "It's not good that he's alone! He needs someone to keep him company."

And so, that night, God made Adam sleep a little deeper. While the man was snoring away, God took one of his ribs and used it to create once more.

When Adam awoke the next morning, he had quite the surprise. "Ishah!" (ee-shah) he exclaimed, when he saw the stunning girl standing nearby. She was stunning with her dark skin, big eyes, and sparkling smile, and she took his breath away.

She was the very first Ishah, the very first woman, and Adam named her "Eve."

Adam wasn't too hard on the eyes either, a regular old prince charming. So Eve happily embraced the handsome man.

You could say Adam and Eve fell madly in love at first sight. Of course, they were the only two people around, so that helped things along.

God watched the two lovebirds gazing into each other's eyes and smiled. This was good.

As time went on, Eve explored the beautiful garden she got to call home. The animals were so friendly and she couldn't get enough of their snuggles.

One day, Eve wandered into the clearing by the tree in the center of the garden.

"Sayyy, Eve," she heard a voice whisper.

"Who's there?" she asked, spinning around to find the source of the voice.

"Is it actually true that God said you can't eat from every tree in this garden?"

Eve's eyes found their mark, a snake that had climbed a nearby tree. "Well hello, Mr. Serpent," she said, smiling at the new friend, "you're very right. God said we can eat the fruit of any of the trees except for this one, the one in the middle. He said not to eat the fruit, or even touch it, or we would die!"

"I say, that doesn't sound right to me. You can eat the fruit of that tree and not die. In fact, God knows that if you eat the fruit, you'll become just like Him. You'll know the difference between good and evil!"

"Truly?" Eve asked, looking at the tree. It was just then that the clouds parted above and a sunray pierced through the leaves to sparkle on a low hanging fruit. "That fruit would be easy enough to pick, and it sure does look tasty," she mused aloud.

She couldn't help noticing that her mouth was watering as she said, "Fruit that makes me wiser and more educated does sound like a good idea, and I'll bet it tastes so very sweet!"

Without even another word from the serpent to encourage her, Eve reached out a hand to pluck the fruit from the tree. She brought it to her lips and took a big bite.

As she was savoring the new flavor, Adam joined her in the clearing. "Eve!" He exclaimed with a worried look.

"Don't worry, dearest, it's delicious!" She said, handing him her leftovers.

He looked at her, and she didn't appear to be dead, so he shrugged and took a big bite. "Yum!" he said around a mouthful.

Eve smiled at Adam, but then she noticed something: he was naked! As she realized this, he noticed her nakedness, too. Suddenly, they were very, very embarrassed.

When God created them, He made them uniquely male and uniquely female. Now that they suddenly realized they didn't have clothes on, and they were very different, they were blushing fiercely.

Quick on her feet, Eve grabbed some leaves from a nearby fig tree and started weaving them together. They were just trying on the new fig leaf clothing when they heard another voice.

This time, it was the voice of God walking in the garden. "Where are you, Adam?" He called out.

Adam grabbed Eve's arm and yanked her behind some bushes, but then thought better of it. After all, God could see through bushes if He wanted to.

Adam stepped out of the bushes and said, "I heard you walking in the garden and was afraid you'd see me because I'm naked. So I hid."

"Who told you that you're naked?" God asked, "Did you eat the fruit I commanded you not to eat?"

Scared, Adam replied, "Well, uh, you know that woman you gave me? Well she gave it to me, and I ate it."

So God asked Eve, "What have you done?"

Eve looked quickly around for her supposed friend, and pointing at him said, "The serpent tricked me, so I ate some of the fruit!"

God then turned his attention to the serpent. God was angry because, although it would take a long time, Adam and Eve would eventually die instead of living forever as He originally planned.

God spoke to the serpent, "Because you've done this, you are cursed. You will crawl on your belly and eat dirt all the days of your life!"

Then God turned to Eve and, because she had shown herself untrustworthy when making the decisions, said, "You must bend your will to your husband's, and he will lead you."

Lastly, God looked at Adam. "Because you listened to your wife, instead of Me, and ate the fruit I commanded you not to eat, you will have to work hard to earn your meals for the rest of your life."

Then God took the skins of animals and made clothes for Adam and Eve, before He led them out of the garden.

God spoke to His creation, "Man now knows good and evil, and so that he doesn't take fruit from the tree of life and live forever in a state that can do evil, it's time for him to go."

So Adam and Eve left the garden of Eden, and God placed angels at the entrance with a flaming sword to guard it.

But though their love story was off to a rough start, it did get better. Adam and Eve lived for almost a thousand years, and during that time they had many, many, many children to brighten their lives.

And out of them came all of us.

Every kind of person, big or small, black or white, came from one woman named Eve.

For the full story, read Genesis 1-5.

WORD SEARCH

```
I A L N C P M Q O T U R X Z
N V I F E U H K I Y O L O N
T E B L Z A R T L S N I S U
H K G A H G F S E R P E N T
E N T M P A D R E Y K P W R
B O D I F R U I T J N O X E
E W T N O D C F S J W M U E
G L Z G R E V E M H I O A B
I E H S B N B R K L A N C B
N D C W I Y S E S D I H E I
N G O O D Q U V T M E G F T
I E S R D A O I A J K H E
N A W D E J U L K M A D A D
G T I X N S S K V L L O P N
```

- EVE
- ADAM
- FIRST
- FRUIT
- GARDEN
- CURSE
- NAKED
- SERPENT
- LIE
- TREE
- ISHAH
- BITE
- ANIMALS
- FORBIDDEN
- IN THE BEGINNING
- FLAMING SWORD
- KNOWLEDGE
- GOOD
- EVIL
- SIN

EVE

SALTED CARAMEL APPLE CIDER PUNCH

INGREDIENTS

- Gallon of Apple Cider
- 2-Liter of Ginger Ale
- Salted Caramel Syrup

INSTRUCTIONS

1. Low boil the Cider in large pot until reduced by a third.
2. Combine the reduced Cider and Ginger Ale in a serving container over ice.
3. Stir in Syrup to taste.
4. Pour and serve!

**For extra pizzazz, pour over ice cream to make a delicious sparkling cider float!

ASENATH

THE STORY OF ASENATH

In Ancient Egypt, there lived a girl named Asenath (Ah-zee-nauth). She was the daughter of the most powerful priest in the Pharaoh's court and lived a life of luxury. She had fancy clothes, furniture, and anything else she could imagine, and she enjoyed every bit of it.

One day, the Pharaoh had a bad dream. When he told his court about the dream, even his wisest men couldn't interpret it. After many failed attempts, someone suddenly remembered that they had a Hebrew slave in prison. He'd interpreted dreams of his fellow prisoners in the past, and everything he said came true.

The Pharaoh summoned this man whose name was Joseph. When Joseph came to the court, the Pharaoh told him what he had dreamed. Joseph immediately knew what it meant and told him that Egypt would have seven years of plenty - the harvests would be massive and it would be a great time! But after those seven years, Egypt would be struck with a famine.

The Pharaoh asked Joseph if anything could be done to change this, but Joseph said no. "The only thing to do, Pharaoh, is to set aside a portion of everything you bring in during the seven years of great harvest. If you do that, you will be able to save enough food to keep everyone fed during the years of famine."

Pharaoh liked the sound of this so much that he made Joseph second in charge over all of Egypt, even ranking higher than Asenath's father. But that wasn't enough to say thanks! So Pharaoh also gave Asenath to Joseph as a wife.

Asenath was shy at first. Her husband was freshly cleaned up and very handsome, and now they were ruling over Egypt. But the two got along well, and soon Joseph became the home Asenath had always wanted.

While she was used to living a fancy life, nothing could've prepared her for the riches around her now. But she noticed that her husband never seemed to care about how much they had, only that they had enough to take care of the people.

As the seven years of feasting went on, Joseph stored away as much as he could. Asenath helped her husband to the best of her ability, and to their great joy, she had two sons along the way. They named their babies Manasseh, meaning "God made me forget all my pain," and Ephraim, meaning "God made me fruitful in the land of my hardship."

Eventually the time of famine came, but Joseph had done well and Egypt had plenty of food stored up. They had so much that word spread to other nations, and people traveled hundreds of miles on foot to buy it.

One day, Joseph came home from work and told Asenath that his brothers were in town. He'd told her in the past how he used to be his father's favorite, and because they were jealous, his brothers had kidnapped him and sold him into slavery. This was how he came to be in Egypt.

Asenath's heart broke for her husband. She knew he missed his family so much, but it was painful to think about them. Now they were in his front yard! To make matters worse, his brothers didn't even recognize him. After so much time had passed, Joseph felt erased.

Joseph didn't go easy on his brothers. He tested them multiple times to see if they were sorry for what they had done. But even as he tested them, he always gave them food from the storehouse.

Finally, Joseph gave a last test and threatened to put their youngest brother in jail. One of his brothers came to him and begged for mercy. He told Joseph that they had already lost one brother through their wrongdoing, and their father wouldn't survive losing another son.

Unable to keep it quiet for a second longer, Joseph told his brother who he was. To Asenath's amazement, the brothers all rejoiced and each took turns apologizing to Joseph.

He gave them more food, then sent them home to get their father. The brothers returned with their father, and the family was fully reunited once more.

Asenath learned so much from her husband about forgiveness and taking care of people in need, and it changed the way she viewed the word "wealthy." Before Joseph, she was wealthy in things. But with Joseph, she was wealthy in family and in love, and her children's names served as a daily reminder of just that!

For the full story, read Genesis 39-50.

WORD SEARCH

```
H A Z P B R O T H E R S Q R
E X S S N S B T Y L I M A F
E J I W X J O C D C B T A A
K W J A A O U Q D O S I O M
S T A L Q S N M P N S H T I
J Q W N B E E A Y V O S J N
T S E I R P G N R I S V K E
O I D U I H Y A A C O N G L
S X D G D R P S M T H U A U
V W I I E A T S I M H Y O R
D T N V H I A A D M O E Y R
Y Z G I F M P H A R A O H U
I F O N A E H Q Y U R A E L
J W V G I E U R I C H E S A
```

- ASENATH
- JOSEPH
- MANASSEH
- EPHRAIM
- PYRAMID
- CONVICT
- PRIEST
- WEDDING
- IN-LAWS
- BROTHERS
- GIVING
- FAMILY
- FAMINE
- PHARAOH
- RICHES
- ROYAL
- BRIDE
- EGYPT
- RULE
- ON

ASENATH

MAKE YOUR OWN HIEROGLYPH

INGREDIENTS

- Cup of Table Salt
- Four Cups of Flour
- One and a Half Cups of Water

TOOLS

- Cookie/biscuit cutter
- Chopstick or butter knife
- String if you wish to use it as an ornament

INSTRUCTIONS

- Mix salt and flour, then slowly add water while kneading the dough.
- Once the dough is smooth and forms a ball, roll it out to roughly 1/2" thickness then use a cookie cutter to shape it.
- Using a chopstick or butter knife, carve an image into the dough, being careful not to cut through the bottom.
- If you plan to use this as an ornament, carve/punch a hole through the top, so that you can loop your string through once dry.
- Bake at 200 degrees for 3-4 hours (until hard and dry) or leave on countertop to air dry for a few days.

THE STORY OF ZIPPORAH

Zipporah was a shepherdess. She loved to watch over her father's sheep as their Midianite family traveled from place to place. They usually lived in a desert place, with little water for the animals and little greenery to admire. But that never bothered her; she was happy.

One day, as she and her sisters were watering their flocks, several mean shepherd men approached the watering hole, "You girls need to get lost. This is our water!"

Zipporah didn't know what to do. There wasn't another watering hole for miles and they still had thirsty sheep on their hands. The sisters had no choice but to listen, as they were very outmatched.

Just as she turned to leave, a man who was lounging under one of the few trees in the area, stood, and came to her side. "What's the problem here?" he asked. "These women are with me, and we are watering our sheep."

The shepherds were happy to pick a fight with women, but this man looked tough. So with a grunt, they said, "Fine, fine, we'll wait."

"I'm Moses," the man said, turning to Zipporah.

She smiled warmly at him, "I'm Zipporah. Thank you for helping us!"

When Zipporah and her sisters got home, they told their father, Jethro, all about the man who had saved the day. "I think he was Egyptian, judging from his clothes," Zipporah said. "Although, his face looked different than the Egyptians we know."

Jethro laughed, "I don't care what he is! He came to my daughters' rescue, and I am in his debt. Why did you leave him behind? Go get him - tell him to join us for dinner."

The daughters hurried back to find Moses. Luckily, he was still by the watering hole. With a short explanation of thanksgiving, they led him back to their dad. Jethro shook hands with the man and offered him a job. Moses gladly accepted.

Moses and Zipporah got along very well. As the days went on, Moses told Zipporah the truth of who he was. He told her that he was actually a Hebrew man, dressed as an Egyptian. His mother was a slave in Egypt, as were the rest of the Hebrews. When the Pharaoh wanted to kill the babies, she'd put him in a basket in the river hoping the waters would carry him to safety.

The water did exactly that and carried baby Moses to the Pharaoh's daughter, who was taking a bath in the river. She immediately adopted him, and he grew up as a prince. Later in life, Moses saw an Egyptian beating up a Hebrew slave, and he couldn't bear to see it. He killed the Egyptian and then fled for his life. That was how he came to be at the watering hole the day he and Zipporah met. He deeply regretted what had happened.

Moses was sweet on Zipporah, and before much time had passed, Jethro gave Zipporah to Moses to be his wife.

They had a baby boy named Eliezer, and Moses took over the shepherding duties so that Zipporah could focus on raising their son.

One day, Moses came home in a tizzy. His face was flushed and his eyes were bright. "Zipporah! We're going to Egypt! God came to me as a voice in a burning bush and told me we must go. He wants to set His people free, and He needs me to lead them to a land He is giving to them."

So, even though she was scared to return to the place from which Moses had fled, Zipporah packed their bags and they hit the road.

The journey took many days and nights. Along the way, God became angry with Moses. There was a ceremony called circumcision that was supposed to take place for all men that served God. Moses hadn't completed the ceremony for his son, and God wasn't happy about it. He was angry that Moses would represent himself as God's spokesperson without following through on the ceremony, so God wanted to kill him.

Zipporah knew why God was angry and performed the ceremony herself. God was pleased. She'd done the right thing when her husband would not, and He decided to give grace to Moses.

It was decided then and there that perhaps it would be better if Zipporah and her son went home, and Moses took on Egypt by himself. The journey was clearly even more dangerous than they expected, and far more demanding of Moses. So the couple parted ways for a while.

Zipporah returned to her father's house and waited for news. As time went on, she heard about the amazing miracles God was working through Moses in Egypt and that Pharaoh had finally agreed to free the Hebrew slaves.

She once again packed her bags and headed out to meet her husband, this time with her father in tow.

When they reunited with Moses, now leading over a million freed slaves, he told them all about what God did for His people. Jethro listened and then exclaimed, "Now I know that the Lord is greater than all gods!"

Zipporah was happy to once again be with her husband, and she joined him as he led God's people home. She happily served the Hebrews alongside her husband as they journeyed through the wilderness towards the promised land.

When Moses' siblings, now freed from Egypt, met Zipporah, they talked about her behind her back. They were frustrated that she wasn't a Hebrew and yet God was using her as Moses' wife. Didn't God use them, too? Why should Zipporah be a ruler over them when she looked different? Why should Moses be in charge when he would choose a wife who wasn't Hebrew?

God heard what Moses' siblings, Aaron and Miriam, were saying about Zipporah and called them out in front of all of Israel. He scolded them for their awful words, then He struck Miriam with leprosy, because she did most of the talking. She said words meant to hurt and eat away at Zipporah, so God gave her a disease that would hurt and eat away at her.

Eventually, Miriam repented and was forgiven and healed. Zipporah knew that the God of her husband was now also the God of her heart, because He had protected her reputation when she didn't even know it was being attacked. Zipporah gave thanks to God and loved Him all the days of her life.

For the full story, ready Exodus 2, 4, and 18, and Numbers 12.

WORD SEARCH

```
T H S M T A V X S H L B I C
W U T E N R H S A A E U N L
A H T S V M I R B Y V R P F
Y S X B D E O H R Z A N Q F
R S H P W P N S D L R I M A
W N I R P S E T E N T N O T
M Z A I C A F F S S P G K S
M T Z N B V C I E G Y U H Y
H V A C D E L K R W G E X D
U C F E I D J K T E E F I W
Q I L E H A M N Y P L E A I
J Z O I F G E Q P J N T G M
I J C O V E N A N T E H O K
T M K A W I L D E R N E S S
```

- ZIPPORAH
- MOSES
- DESERT
- SHEEP
- BURNING
- TRAVEL
- PRINCE
- SAVED
- WRATH
- SEVEN
- EGYPT
- STAFF
- WATER
- FLOCK
- WILDERNESS
- COVENANT
- PACK
- TENT
- FIRE
- WIFE

ZIPPORAH

SHEEP PUPPET

TOOLS

- Paper
- Cotton Balls
- Popsicle Stick
- Scissors
- Marker
- Glue

INSTRUCTIONS

- Cut out one large oval, one medium, and one small.
- Cut out two rectangles for legs.
- Glue large oval to popsicle stick, then glue the pieces together to create the shape of a sheep (see picture to the right).
- Draw eyes and a smile.
- Glue cotton balls on the body to create fluff.
- Tah dah! You've got a sheep puppet!

RAHAB

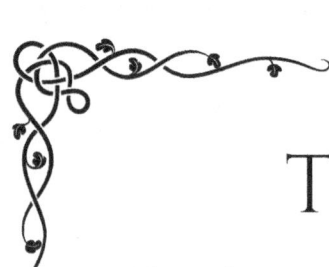

THE STORY OF RAHAB

When the Israelites left Egypt, Moses led them to a new land that was promised to them by God. But before they could enter the land, they had some work to do. First, they had to clear out the wicked people who were living there and doing evil things to hurt each other.

Moses was very old, so he gave the leadership title to Joshua and retired to the mountains. Joshua was a hearty warrior who didn't shy away from the task of conquering new lands. He sent spies into the promised land to check on the layout of things and come up with a plan to take it over.

The Israelites were a massive traveling party - there were over a million of them! So news about them spread through all the cities, and especially in a nearby city called Jericho. Jericho just so happened to be smack-dab in the middle of where God wanted the Israelites to live, and it was full of some very strong and wicked men. The Israelites needed to know if a battle was necessary to drive out the evil.

When the spies arrived, they met a woman named Rahab. She was a woman who lived a very bad lifestyle; she would pretend to be the girlfriend of any man who paid her, whether he was single or married! But Rahab knew her lifestyle was wrong, so she was working hard to change it. She had a business idea to make clothes and had the materials on her rooftop.

Rahab knew that people would be looking for the spies, so she took them up to the roof and hid them under the giant mounds of flax she was turning into thread for clothes.

News spread quickly through Jericho that the spies had met Rahab and were hanging out at her house. When someone told the king, he was angry and immediately sent a soldier to Rahab's front door.

The soldier knocked on the door. When Rahab opened it to see who it was, he said, "By order of the king: bring out the men who are staying with you, for they're Israelites searching out the land to conquer us!"

Rahab batted her lashes and, mustering all her beauty and wits, told the soldier,"Oh sir, it's true that I had men staying with me! But I didn't know where

they came from, and when I told them that the city gate was to be shut at dark, they left. I don't know where they went, but I bet if you go after them right now, you can catch them!"

The soldier wasted no time in gathering his fellow soldiers and ran off into the night to find the spies. They left the city, the gate slamming firmly shut behind them, and went so far as the Jordan River! Of course, they didn't find the spies way out there, as the spies were still safely tucked away on Rahab's rooftop.

Back at her house, Rahab went upstairs to talk to the spies. "I know that the Lord has given you our land. Everyone is afraid of you, and as you enter a new kingdom, the people living there flee.

"We heard about Egypt: how God delivered you out as freed slaves and did many, many miracles along the way, even drying up the Red Sea for you to walk over! And we heard that you've conquered our neighbors by the river, and completely destroyed them. No one has any courage left here, because they fear you and your God. He is definitely God in Heaven above and on Earth below.

"So please, I beg of you, swear to me by the name of the Lord that, since I have been good to you, you will also be good to me and my family. Please give me a sure sign that you will save my family, my father, mother, brothers, and sisters. Please keep us alive when you conquer this city, too."

The spies smiled warmly at this woman who had risked everything to keep them safe. "We owe you our lives!" they exclaimed. "If you don't tell anyone what we've been up to, when the Lord gives us this land, we will be kind and faithful to you and your family."

Rahab was relieved. She led them across the rooftop to the city wall that was connected to her house. There was a window in the wall there, and she threw a rope through it to let the spies climb down.

She turned to the spies and said, "Go now, but run into the hills away from the river or the soldiers will find you. Everyone knows that your people are camping on the other side of the water, so that's definitely where they'll be looking. Hide in the hills for three days until the soldiers have returned, then go on your way."

One of the spies handed her a scarlet cord and said, "We will honor what we've said. When we come into this land, you are to tie this scarlet cord in this very window, then gather your family and wait. If anyone leaves your house and goes into the street, their death will be on their own head, and it won't be our fault. But if you tell anyone about this, this promise is canceled."

Rahab nodded eagerly, "Exactly as you've said it, so be it!"

The spies went through the window, scaled down the wall, and fled into the night.

Not wasting any time, Rahab tied the scarlet cord in the window, and set about gathering her family to wait. And wait. And wait. And wait.

Days turned to weeks, and weeks turned to months. Then one day, Rahab looked out her window to see a million Israelites marching silently around the city.

Six days in a row, the Israelites marched a single lap around the city in absolute silence. Rahab and her family sat nervously in the house. What would become of them?

Then, on the seventh day, the sound of trumpets pierced the air. Rahab rushed to the window just in time to see the Israelites lift their fists into the air and SHOUT!

The shout continued for what seemed like hours, but was actually merely a minute, and the walls of the city trembled, shook, and fell flat!

The Israelites rushed into the now wall-less city and easily conquered the people.

But! Just as the spies had said, Rahab and her family were safe, because when the walls fell, her home alone stayed standing. The scarlet cord was still dancing in the breeze.

Joshua met with Rahab and thanked her for her bravery in hiding his spies. He was impressed by her desire to know the God of the Israelites and taught her their ways.

Rahab became a dear friend to all of the Israelites, a heroine of sorts for her courageous act. She happily lived out her days with them, rejoicing because she now knew the God of the Israelites and served Him, too.

For the full story, read Joshua 2-6.

RAHAB

WORD SEARCH

```
M A R C H I N G B F E B Y X
O W P Q L M C O L H C J T T
B A N P F A K S E V E N A
R I C T A G D Y R D L R H L
T T R U M P E T S R W I T F
T S S D I L B I A E O C V L
H X O F L I V C O R D H U L
W G L K Y T S Q J F N O W E
J Q D N D I H P S K I R G F
Y M I I J Q O R I L W A L L
R V E S A E U U L E M H N A
U Z R L E X T W E P S A O X
S P S O O K Z A N J I B Z A
P A T I E N T X T M N C G D
```

- RAHAB
- SCARLET
- WINDOW
- SPIES
- PATIENT
- JERICHO
- FAMILY
- SOLDIERS
- TRUMPET
- SILENT
- SEVEN
- FELL FLAT
- SHOUT
- WAIT
- MARCHING
- FLAX
- CORD
- WALL
- CITY
- HID

SCARLET CORD

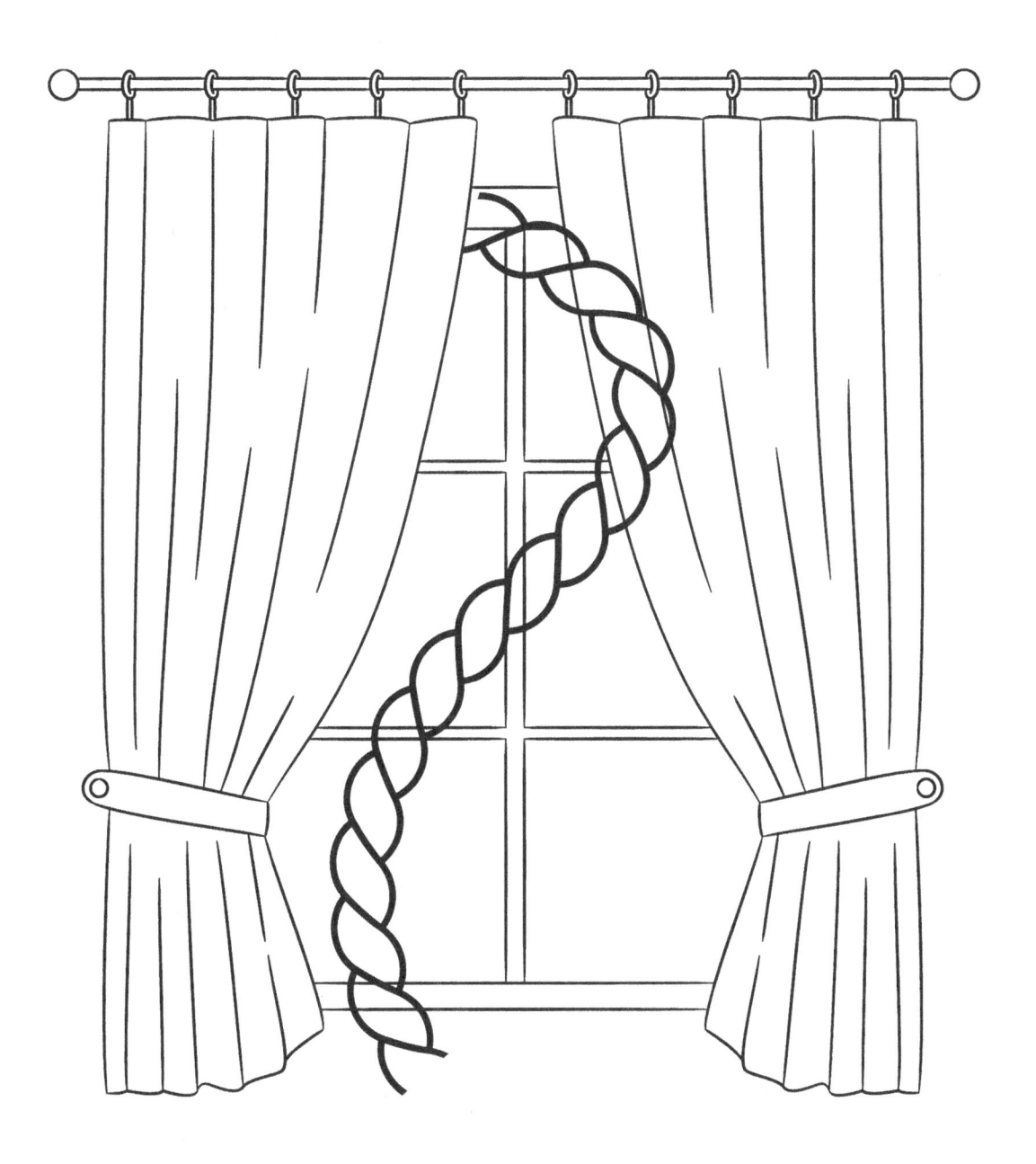

Braid red yarn to make a cord, then hang it from your window like Rahab!

DEBORAH

THE STORY OF DEBORAH

In the days when Israelites couldn't decide whether or not to serve God, He sent Judges to guide them back to Him. When they were especially naughty, evil kings would take over their lands and make them miserable.

It was during the reign of a terrible king named Jabin that a girl became Judge. Her name was Deborah, and because of her kindness and wisdom, God chose to speak to her.

Deborah would leave the city and sit under her favorite palm tree in the hills. There, people would come with their problems and worries, and God would tell her how to fix them.

One day, Deborah asked for her friend Barak to come for a visit. When he came to see her, she said, "Barak, didn't God tell you to gather up your men and take 10,000 soldiers to face the wicked king's army in battle? He will give you the victory."

Barak liked the idea of victory, but even with 10,000 men to back him up, he was scared. He thought about it for a moment, then said, "I'll tell you what, Deb. If you will come with me, I'll go. But if you're not going, neither am I."

Barak was probably thinking that since Deborah was God's close friend, God would make sure she, and all who were with her, made it home safe.

Deborah answered him, "Okay, Barak. I will go with you. But, since you won't go at the command of God unless I go with you, the Lord will defeat the evil king's captain, Sisera, through a woman. You will not get the glory."

Sad to not get the credit, but relieved to have her with him, Barak mounted his horse alongside Deborah. They rode quickly to the meeting place and gathered their army.

When word reached the evil Captain Sisera that the Israelites were gathering to fight, he put together his best warriors and took 900 iron chariots to meet them head on.

As the enemy approached, Deborah called to Barak, "Rise up! This is the day that the Lord will give you victory; doesn't He go before you?"

Barak heard the call and charged. Swords clashed, arrows flew, and it was over as quick as it began. The Lord gave the victory to Barak. Not a soldier of Sisera's was still standing, and the evil captain fled for his life.

Deborah and Barak sang a song of great joy, and shouted, "March on, my soul, with might!"

They rejoiced for God had once again delivered His people.

Deborah happily went back to her favorite palm tree and continued to lead Israel for the rest of her days.

For the full story, read Judges 4-5.

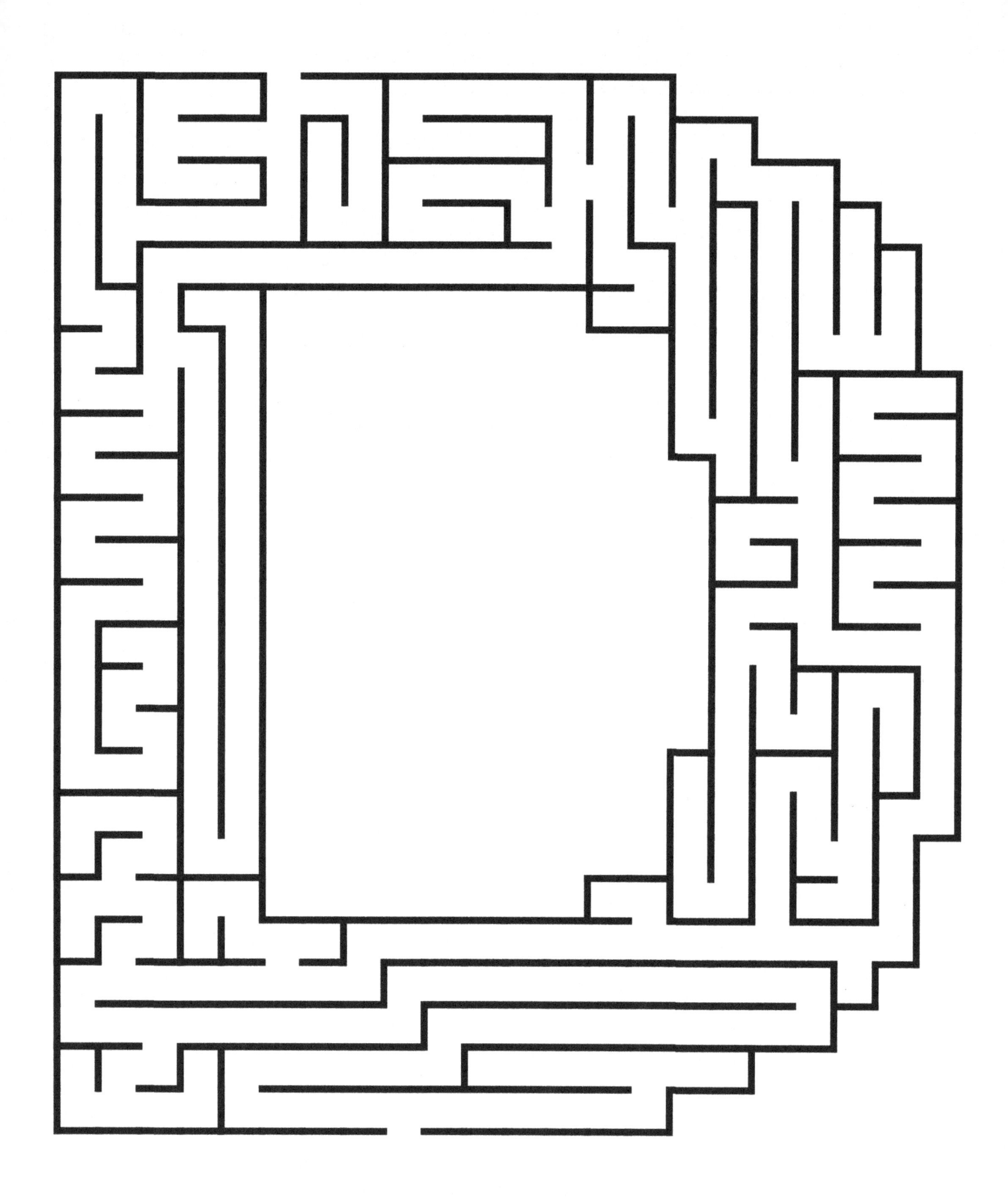

DEBORAH

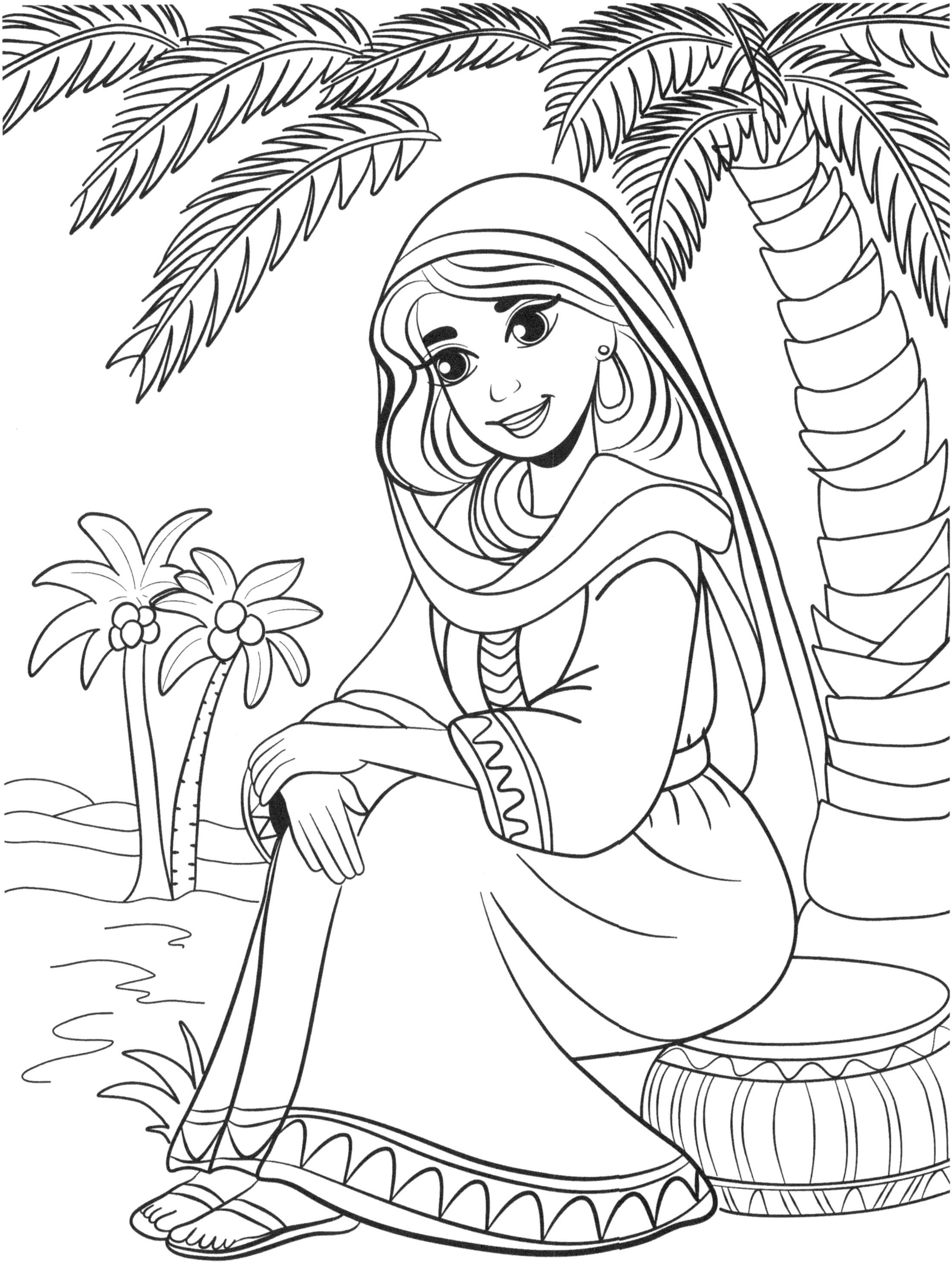

WORD SEARCH

```
A L E S N U O C S R E F Q P
X K G G J B D M O E F G I N
T B J N S H I E L D S R B A
K F U R D I M T C A N T W R
E L D O C D T A B I H P W G
U Z G E W A R W E C D O Y U
U V E E B T U V K W V E Q M
N K I R S O P A L M T R E E
R A J S Q P R O P H E S Y N
S I M W R A C A L L O N P T
C H A O B A G C H A R I O T
S U J R W L E H F Y X O I H
A E L D J K I L E A D E R T
B N O L M D Z M Q N L U Z X
```

- DEBORAH
- BARAK
- PALM TREE
- BATTLE
- JUDGE
- CALL ON
- ISRAEL
- SWORD
- SHIELD
- CHARIOT
- ARGUMENT
- DECIDE
- LEADER
- WOMAN
- PROPHESY
- COUNSEL
- GOD
- BEE
- WAR
- SIT

STICK SWORDS

Make a sword out of sticks and yarn, then practice fighting to join Deborah's army!

JAEL

THE STORY OF JAEL

When the evil Captain Sisera lost the battle against Israel, he knew he needed to hide. It was just his luck that as he was running, he came to his friend Heber's home.

Covered in mud and exhausted, he hurried to the tent and called out, "Heber, are you home?"

A woman peeked out from the tent entrance, "Who's there?"

"Hello, Jael," Sisera said, recognizing the woman as Heber's wife. "I'm a friend of your husband's. Is he home?"

Jael took in his messy appearance and realized he must be fleeing the battle she'd heard was raging. She knew he must have lost and the Israelites would be in hot pursuit. That would be just like Sisera. As long as Jael had known him, he was a very mean man. Of course he wouldn't stay and fight beside his soldiers. Instead, he left them to die and ran away like a chicken.

Suddenly, Jael had an idea, "He's not here, but please do come inside! Don't be afraid, I'll take care of you!"

Sisera followed her inside and barked, "Get me something to drink, I'm thirsty!" Then he plopped down onto a cushion.

"Of course!" Jael rushed to a nearby pitcher and poured him a glass of milk. It was still warm, fresh from the cows.

Sisera chugged the drink, then laid down. "I'm going to sleep. You keep watch and if anyone asks you if someone is here, you better tell them no!"

"Of course, sir," Jael said, and covered him with a rug. "I'll just hide you under here, so no one will find you."

Sisera's eyes were getting heavy. He was so tired and the milk was sitting heavy in his stomach. It wasn't long before he drifted off to dreamland.

Once he was in a deep sleep, Jael set about her plan. She grabbed a tent peg and hammer, snuck over to the evil king, and drove the nail right through his temple! He was nailed to the ground, never to awake.

Jael heard a commotion and went outside to find the Israelite army, led by Barak, standing at her doorstep. The good guys had won, and she'd helped finish it. "Come inside, sir!" She said to Barak, waving her hand toward the entrance, "I have something to show you!"

When Barak entered the tent and found the evil captain stuck in place, he knew that Deborah's prophecy had been fulfilled. God had defeated Sisera through a woman, and the glory would be hers forever.

He gave her a firm handshake and a clap on the back. "Good work, Jael!" He said. "This evil man will never hurt another person!"

Jael smiled, "God's people will always have the final victory!"

For the full story, read Judges 4-5.

WORD SEARCH

```
J A D E T S U A H X E R F D
A G E U L V I C T O R Y L R
C A P T N E O V O F L C E A
G L E P A C S E Q V L B E R
R H R X S H O W V D E A T K
K R U D H A Q U R L X R E A
E L N P G S E A C R L A E T
O A I A M E U S R U G K K D
E S A M T G N J A E L V C H
S T T X D K N U P N S A U U
C E P N C P G E T W X I T Q
K N A S L E E P E Y E L S V
D T C O N Y R E N D D P X W
S C H A T S T A H A M M E R
```

- JAEL
- BARAK
- CAPTAIN
- SISERA
- SWEET
- ASLEEP
- VICTORY
- ESCAPE
- CHASE
- COVERED
- STAND GUARD
- STUCK
- SHOW
- EXHAUSTED
- HAMMER
- FLEE
- MILK
- TENT
- RUG
- PEG

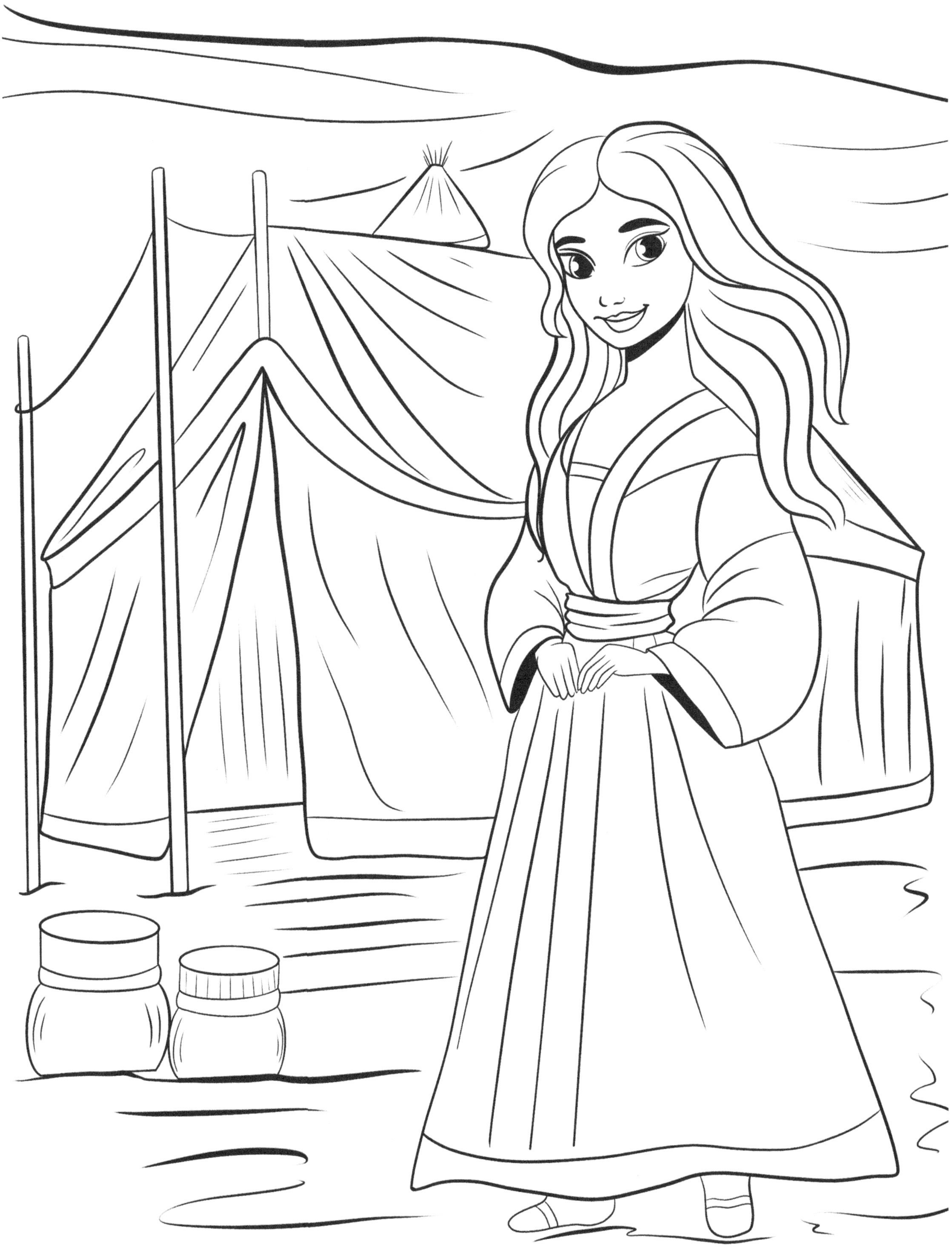

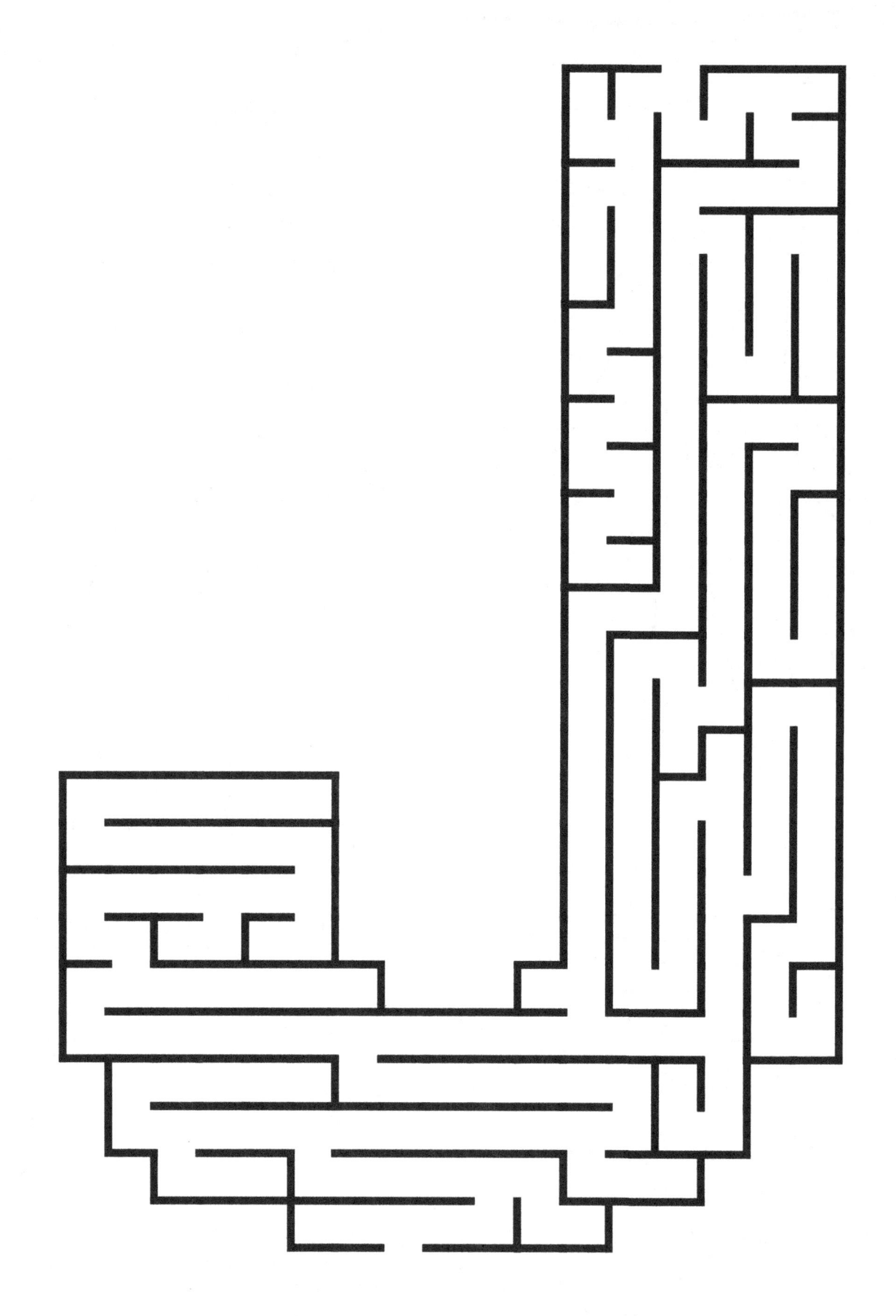

JAEL

SPICED CITRUS TEA

INGREDIENTS

- 6 Cups of Water
- 1 Teaspoon of Whole Cloves
- 1 Cinnamon Stick
- 6 Lipton Black Tea Bags
- 3/4 Cup of Orange Juice
- 1/2 Cup of Cane Sugar
- 1/4 Cup of Pinneapple Juice
- 2 Tablespoons of Lemon Juice

INSTRUCTIONS

- Combine water, cloves, cinnamon, and tea bags in a pot. Bring to a boil and steep.
- In a separate pot, combine juice and sugar. Allow to boil to fully dissolve sugar.
- Pour tea into juice mixture, being sure to strain out cloves, cinnamon, and tea bags.
- Serve hot with your favorite pastry!

DELILAH

THE STORY OF DELILAH

Sometime after Deborah judged the people of Israel, God raised up a new leader named Samson. Samson was a miracle child because he was born to barren parents. They dedicated him to the Lord, and he took a vow called the Nazarite vow.

Samson didn't drink wine, touch dead animals, or cut his hair. Because he lived sacrificially for God, God gave him superhuman strength.

While he judged Israel, Samson single-handedly killed thousands of Philistines who were persecuting the Israelites.

One day, Samson met a woman called Delilah.

Delilah was beautiful, smart, and had a nice house. In no time at all, Samson was head over heels for her! He was as in love with her as a man could be, but unfortunately, Delilah didn't feel the same way.

The Philistines knew this was the case, so they met with Delilah and offered her 1,100 pieces of silver if she would help them capture him. They had learned their lesson about challenging Samson - the man was strong enough to kill 3,000 of their soldiers with nothing but a donkey's jawbone! They were no match for him. But perhaps Delilah would be.

Delilah liked the idea of becoming 1,100 pieces of silver richer. The next time Samson came to visit, she cuddled up close and said, "Sweet honeyboo, please tell me how you are so strong. Is there anything that can bind you up or keep you down?"

Samson laughed, finding her question odd, but cute. "Yes, dear. In fact, if someone were to bind my hands with seven brand new bowstrings, then I would be just as weak as any other man!"

Delilah got word to the Philistines what he'd said and that night, when Samson was sawing logs, they brought her seven bowstrings. Then they hid in the house while she got to work.

Delilah crept to Samson's side and tied him up with the bowstrings. Then she stepped back and in her best actress voice, she cried out, "Samson! Wake up! The Philistines are upon you!"

Samson bolted right up and immediately snapped the bowstrings as he pulled his hands apart. "What?! Where are they?" He thundered, then began to calm when he realized the only other person in the room was Delilah.

"Oh, Samson, how could you lie to me?" She asked, walking toward him, "I just wanted to test what you said was true, and it wasn't!"

Samson laughed again at her antics. What a sweetly odd woman. "Darling Delilah, I'm sorry I lied. All you actually have to do is tie me up with new ropes that have never been used, and I'll be just like everyone else."

The two went back to bed and then enjoyed a beautiful day together. The next night, once Samson was again fast asleep, the Philistines brought new ropes to Delilah and hid.

She once again crept to his side, tied him up, then cried out, "Samson - the Philistines are upon you! Wake up!"

Once again, Samson jumped to his feet and easily snapped the ropes.

Delilah threw her hands into the air and shouted, "You lied, AGAIN!"

With another chuckle, Samson patted Delilah on the shoulder. This was becoming quite the little game between them. "Yes, I lied. But here is the honest truth, if you tightly weave my long hair into a loom, I will be just like everyone else."

The next time night fell, Delilah had the necessary tool on hand. So the very moment Samson's eyes were shut and his snoring started up, she wove his hair tightly into a loom, then cried out, "Samson, awake! The Philistines are here!"

Of course, Samson woke, stood to his feet, and the loom snapped in two.

Delilah burst into tears. "How can you say you love me if you won't even trust me with your heart? You lie to me to poke fun at me, and won't tell me the true secret of your strength! You don't love me at all!"

Samson realized then that this wasn't a joke, so the two eventually went to sleep without him concocting another story.

But there would be no peace for Samson. Day after day after day, Delilah begged him for the secret. The nagging was nonstop and Samson was beginning to feel crazy, so he finally snapped. "Okay, Delilah! I will tell you, just stop bugging me!"

Delilah eagerly came to his side, "Go on!"

Samson sighed then said, "The true secret of my strength is a vow I made to God. A razor has never touched my head, and if my hair is ever cut, the strength of God would leave me."

This time, Delilah believed him. She could tell it was the truth. So she sent word to the Philistine soldiers to come that night and be ready.

When Samson began to feel sleepy that evening, Delilah told him to rest his head on her lap. He snuggled up with the love of his life, closed his eyes, and went to sleep.

The door opened as a man crept into the house. He was the local barber, and he made quick work of chopping off all of Samson's hair.

One last time, Delilah cried out, "Samson, wake up! The Philistines are upon you!"

This time, when Samson woke up, he realized that he didn't have his strength anymore. He raised his hands to his head and felt nothing but skin. "Oh Delilah, what did you do?" He asked as the Philistines ran in from the other room and grabbed him.

They dragged him out of Delilah's house, leaving her to count her stacks of silver.

Even though Samson was now destined to live as a slave to the Philistines, and even though they gouged his eyes out and he lived the rest of his life blind, God did not forget Samson. Samson got to partner with God one final time.

The Philistines threw a party to celebrate their victories and brought Samson out to brag about how they had defeated the superhuman. While they partied, Samson asked a little servant boy to lead him to the two pillars that were holding up the house.

Samson placed a hand on each pillar and prayed that God would give him strength one last time. "Let me get vengeance for my eyes, and let me die with the Philistines," he said, then heaved with all his might.

God granted his request and gave Samson the strength he needed to push over the two pillars. The house caved in and more Philistines died with Samson that day than all he had killed before combined.

And perhaps he even took Delilah with them.

For the full story, read Judges 16

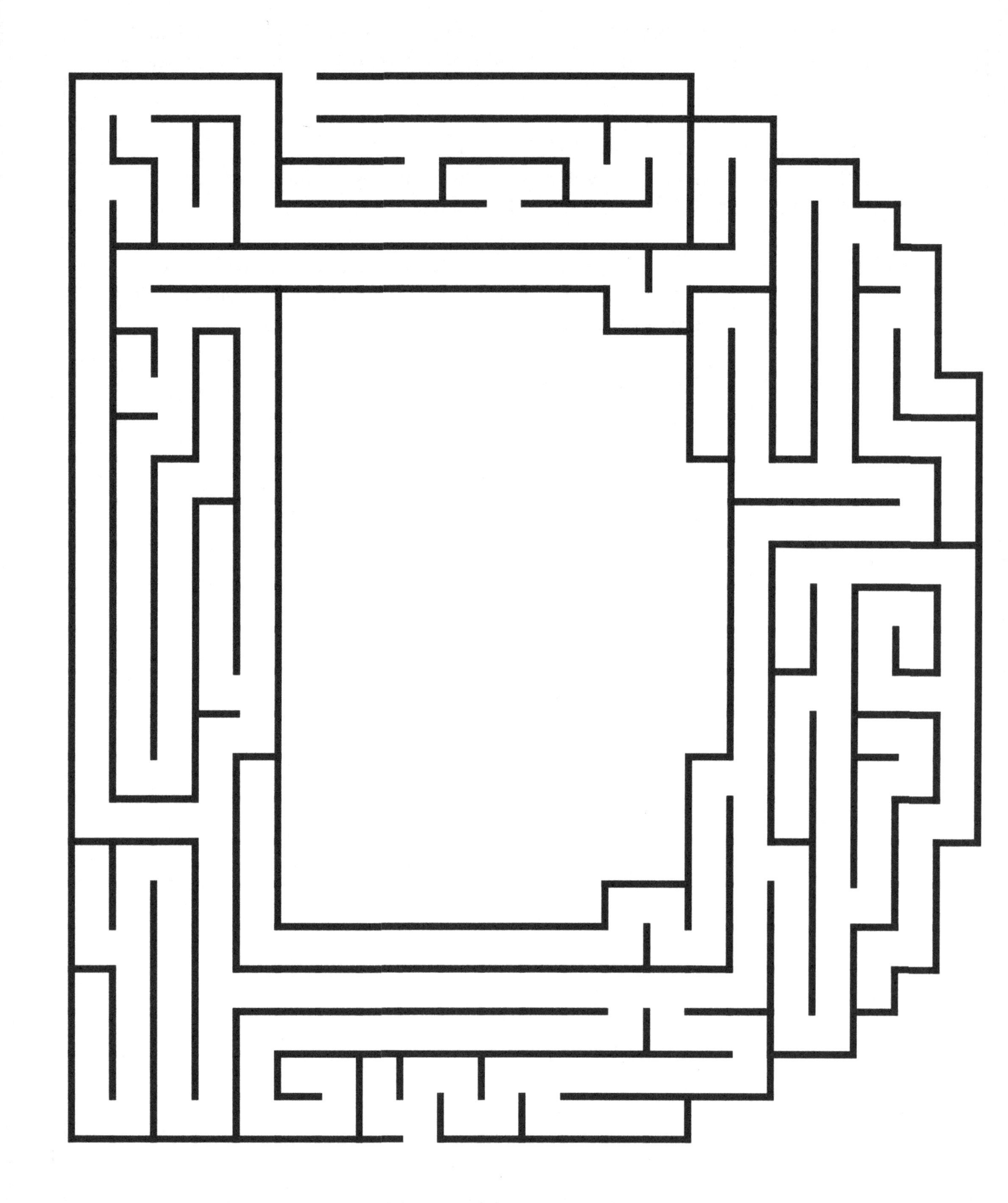

DELILAH

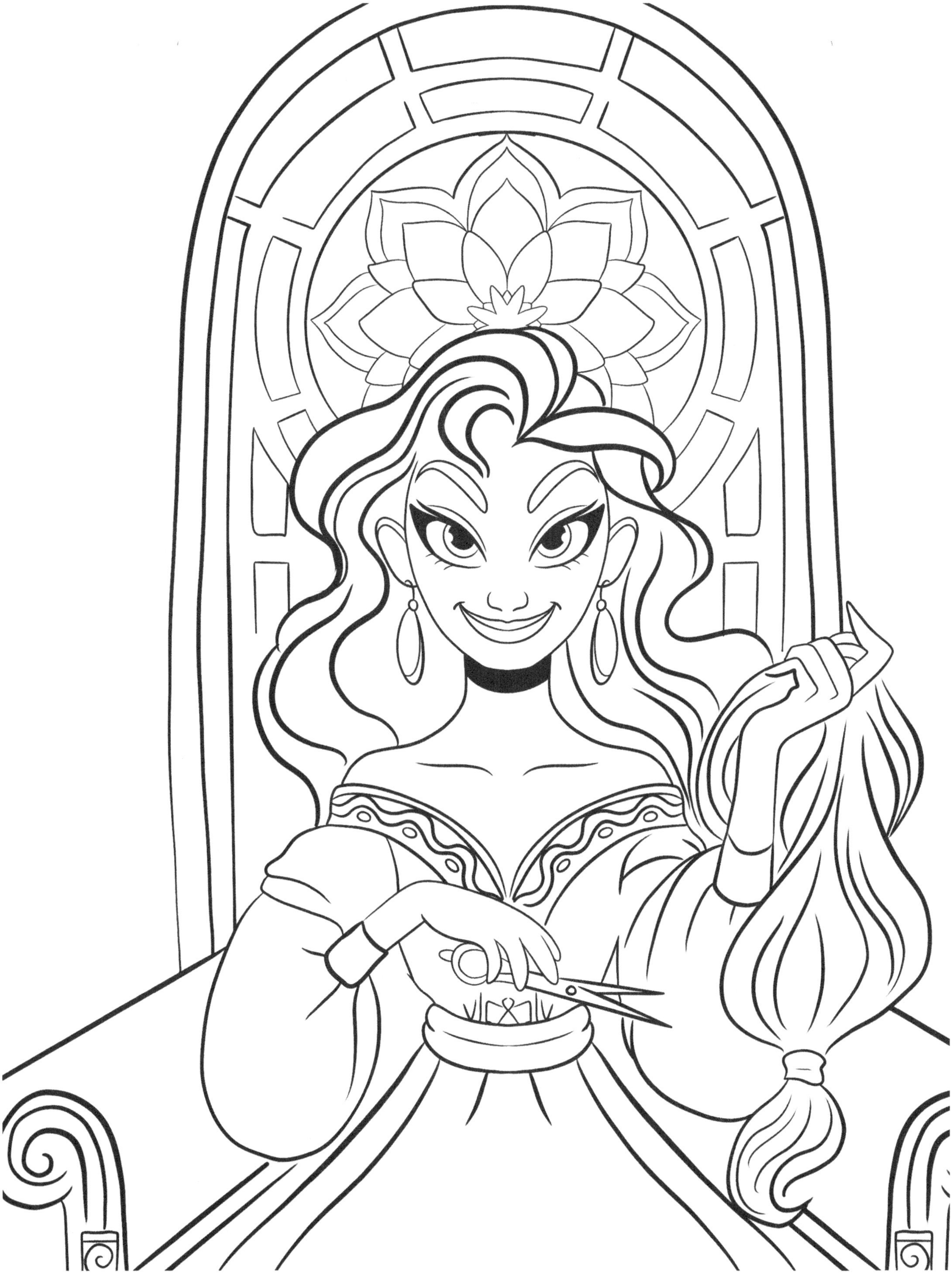

WORD SEARCH

```
K L J O M V W C P E N B J F
M L P N A Z A R I T E K U V
H E I L P O V F D O G I G E
I N L O X U W S T Y T D H P
A E L D N U O B O P I A L H
Y J A E E R V N Q P J E G I
T R R C N L S S E K A C X L
U E S E O R I E M D L X B I
A B B I S U L L O V E F W S
E R D V M S V H A I R C U T
B A W E A V E A C H E O A I
W B O W S T R I N G S Z P N
X H Y V R K U T M Q S L Z E
Z X I T S T R E N G T H A S
```

- DELILAH
- SAMSON
- SILVER
- HAIRCUT
- PHILISTINES
- DECEIVE
- NAZARITE
- STRENGTH
- BOWSTRINGS
- BEAUTY
- BARBER
- ASLEEP
- PLEAD
- PILLARS
- VALLEY
- WEAVE
- ROPE
- LOVE
- BOUND
- VOW

PIN THE HAIR ON SAMSON

How to Play:

- Print out a picture of a man's silhouette and tape it to the wall.
- Print and cut out braids (like above), then add a piece of tape (or a stick pin if old enough) to the top.
- Take turns wearing a blindfold and trying to tape the braids on Samson's head. Closest placement to a natural hairline wins!
- For extra difficulty, take a spin once blindfolded before you try to pin the braid!

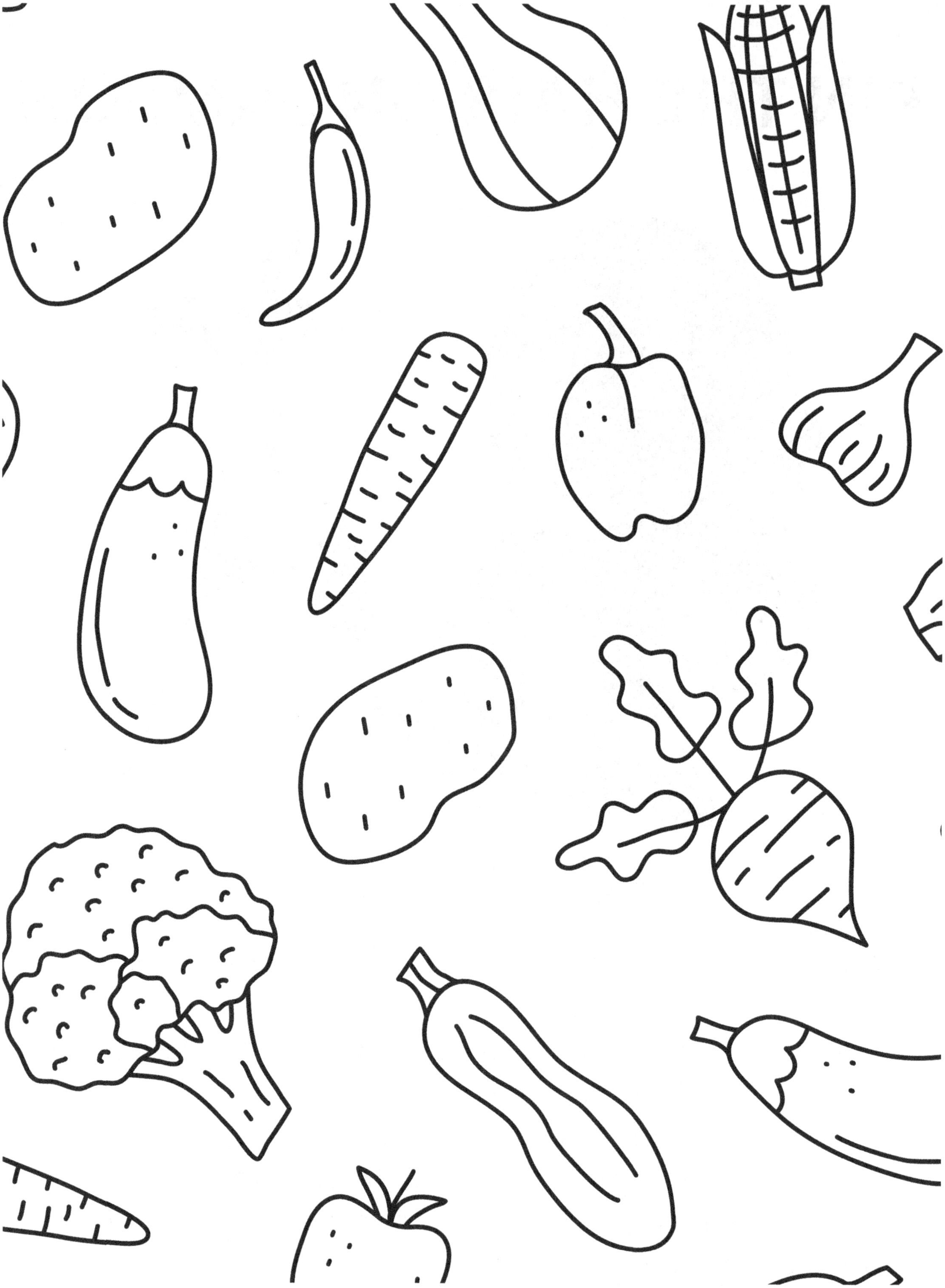

ABIGAIL

THE STORY OF ABIGAIL

Before David was the king of Israel, he lived as an outlaw in the wilderness, on the run from his predecessor, King Saul. Hundreds of strong men followed him into the wild, and together they defended the Israelite people from enemies.

There was a man named Nabal nearby. He was very wealthy and had three thousand sheep and a thousand goats! Because he lived on the outskirts, robbers would often try to help themselves to his animals for food. So David and his men started protecting Nabal's flock.

Nabal was an awful man. He was known for being harsh and brutish. But he had a beautiful wife named Abigail, and all who knew her, loved her. Her ability to discern right from wrong would often help heal the rifts caused by his rude nature.

One day, after many weeks of protecting Nabal's flock, David sent ten young men to greet Nabal with a message.

They came to Nabal and, after some small talk, said, "We're David's men and we've been watching over your shepherds and protecting your flock. We hope this will make us favorable to you and ask that you provide us with some food? Today is a holiday, and we'd really like to participate in the feast!"

When Nabal heard this, he laughed in their faces. "Who is David? There are many servants these days who leave their masters and find themselves in need. Should I give my bread, water, and meat to men who come from who knows where?"

The group returned to David to let him know what Nabal had said. David was outraged. "Every man strap on his sword!" He yelled to his men.

So four hundred men did exactly that and followed David as he charged toward Nabal's home.

Meanwhile at Nabal's house, one of his shepherds came running up to Abigail completely flustered and out of breath. He told Abigail everything that had happened, saying, "David sent messengers to greet our master and he railed at them! But David's men were so good to us. They protected us and helped us keep track of our sheep and goats. As long as we were with them, we suffered no harm. They were like a wall around us, day and night! Please consider what you should do, because they will now surely harm us all, and our master is such a worthless man that he won't listen to us!"

Upon hearing this, Abigail wasted no time. She worked quickly with her servants to gather two hundred loaves of bread, two skins of wine, five butchered sheep, two bushels of grain, a hundred clusters of raisins, and two hundred cakes of figs. She was determined to give David and his men a great feast! They packed up the food and loaded it onto donkeys. Then, realizing it would take her too long to get to David, Abigail said to the shepherds, "Go ahead of me, I'm right behind you!"

Abigail hopped onto a donkey, grabbed the reins of the other donkeys, and followed her men. She didn't even stop to tell her husband, just made her way as quickly as possible.

As David and his men came down from the mountain, they met Abigail in the valley. David was still furious and said, "We've guarded all that this man has in vain. Nothing of his was missed, and he has returned to me evil for good. May God strike down any man of Nabal's that I leave alive by morning!"

Abigail shuddered at his words. This outlaw was fierce, and she had every reason to be terrified. She jumped down from her donkey and rushed to him, throwing herself down at his feet.

Then Abigail made the speech she had been practicing on the ride over: "On me alone, my lord, be the guilt. Please let me speak, and please hear me. Don't even think about the worthless Nabal; his name means 'stupid,' and that's what he is. I wasn't there when your messengers arrived, but I heard what was said. Please know that God wants to keep you from the guilt of Nabal's blood by saving him from your hand. Let your enemies and all who do evil against you be just like Nabal - a fool.

"And here, I've brought this present for you and your men. Please forgive me for the way I've wronged you. The Lord will certainly bless you because you are doing His work, and you will never do anything evil as long as you live.

"If men try to kill you, you will be spared by the Lord and your enemies will fail. You will be appointed king of Israel, and when God has done you this good, you will remember me."

David was floored by what Abigail had said. She was right. Though Nabal had done a great evil by not rewarding him for protecting his flock, killing Nabal and his household would be wrong.

So David called off his men and told Abigail, "Blessed be the God of Israel who sent you to meet me. Blessed be your discretion, and blessed be you, because you have saved me from making a bad decision that would have made me evil, too. If you had not come and spoken these things, by morning there would not be a single man left standing in Nabal's house."

Abigail breathed a heavy sigh of relief. Her people were saved!

She then pulled the reins of the donkeys forward and offered her many gifts to David and his men.

As the men began to feast, David told Abigail to return home in peace. "I will obey your voice and grant your request."

When she got home, Abigail found Nabal drunk out of his mind. She didn't say anything to him until the sun came up and he was a little more sober to hear her.

She sat down across from him at breakfast and told him the story, that David was set out to kill him and that she had taken a feast to apologize for her husband's wicked behavior.

When Nabal heard the last of the tale, he had a heart attack. For nine days he stayed alive, but he was in a coma. Then on the tenth day, God struck Nabal and he died.

When David heard the news of Nabal's death, he said, "Blessed be the Lord for avenging me, and for saving me from my own wrongdoing. The Lord has placed the evil of Nabal on his own head."

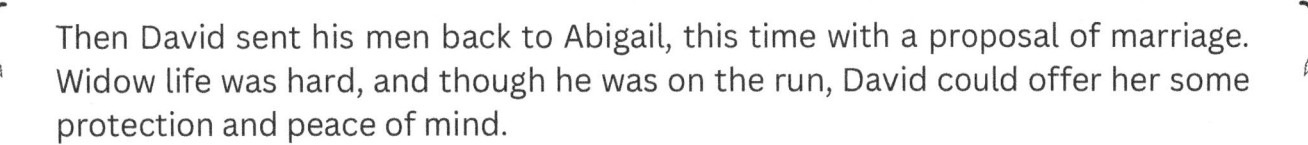

Then David sent his men back to Abigail, this time with a proposal of marriage. Widow life was hard, and though he was on the run, David could offer her some protection and peace of mind.

Abigail bowed before his men and said, "I am your handmaid, a servant to wash the feet of my Lord's servants."

Then she rose and went to find her donkey, before heading off into the sunset and to her new life as the outlaw's wife.

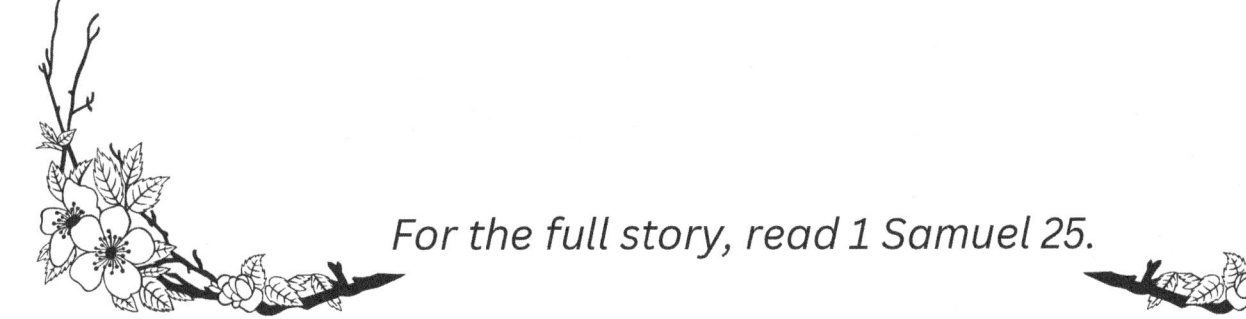

For the full story, read 1 Samuel 25.

WORD SEARCH

```
D I S C E R N I N G F B I L
A U B R E A D N A E H E G J
S C Y A B I G A I L C A V E
O W R I P F C B D G M U K N
M P R S O W D A V I D T N O
X Q O E N A O L T F O I P T
B S S N M S N U S T Q F S S
Y A H S B T K R T S T U U T
X G P R O T E C T L R L V R
I O I L J O Y G H I A A W O
P D J V L K Q J P F B W Z K
E Z F E S T N A V R E S C E
W O C O M P A S S I O N E Y
N S T R O K A M I U V N D X
```

- ABIGAIL
- NABAL
- DAVID
- RAISENS
- BREAD
- GIFTS
- DONKEY
- PROTECT
- OUTLAW
- SERVANTS
- FEAST
- DISCERNING
- BEAUTIFUL
- SORRY
- COMPASSION
- CAVE
- STONE
- STROKE
- BRIDE
- JOY

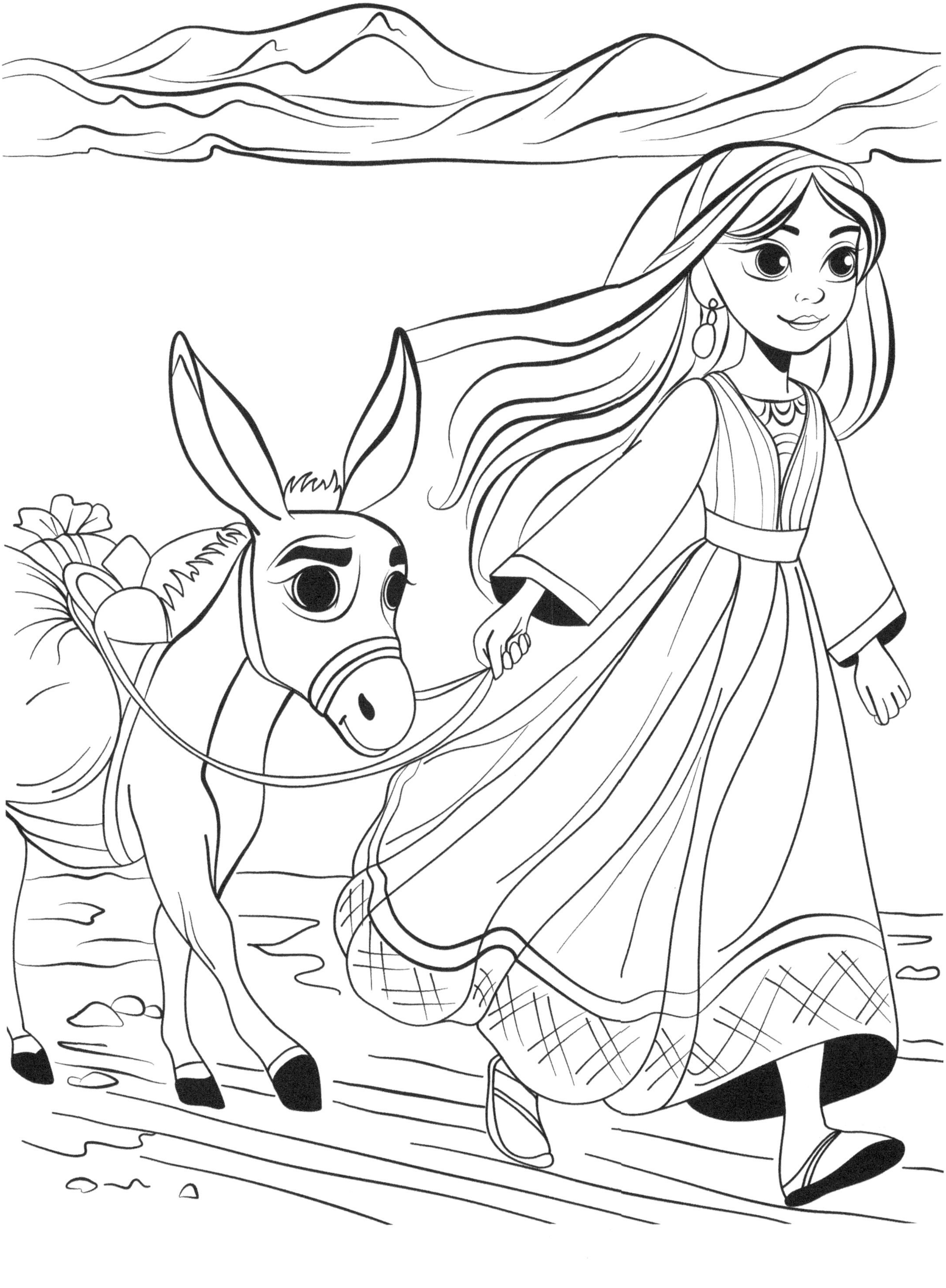

ABIGAIL

SHARE A FEAST

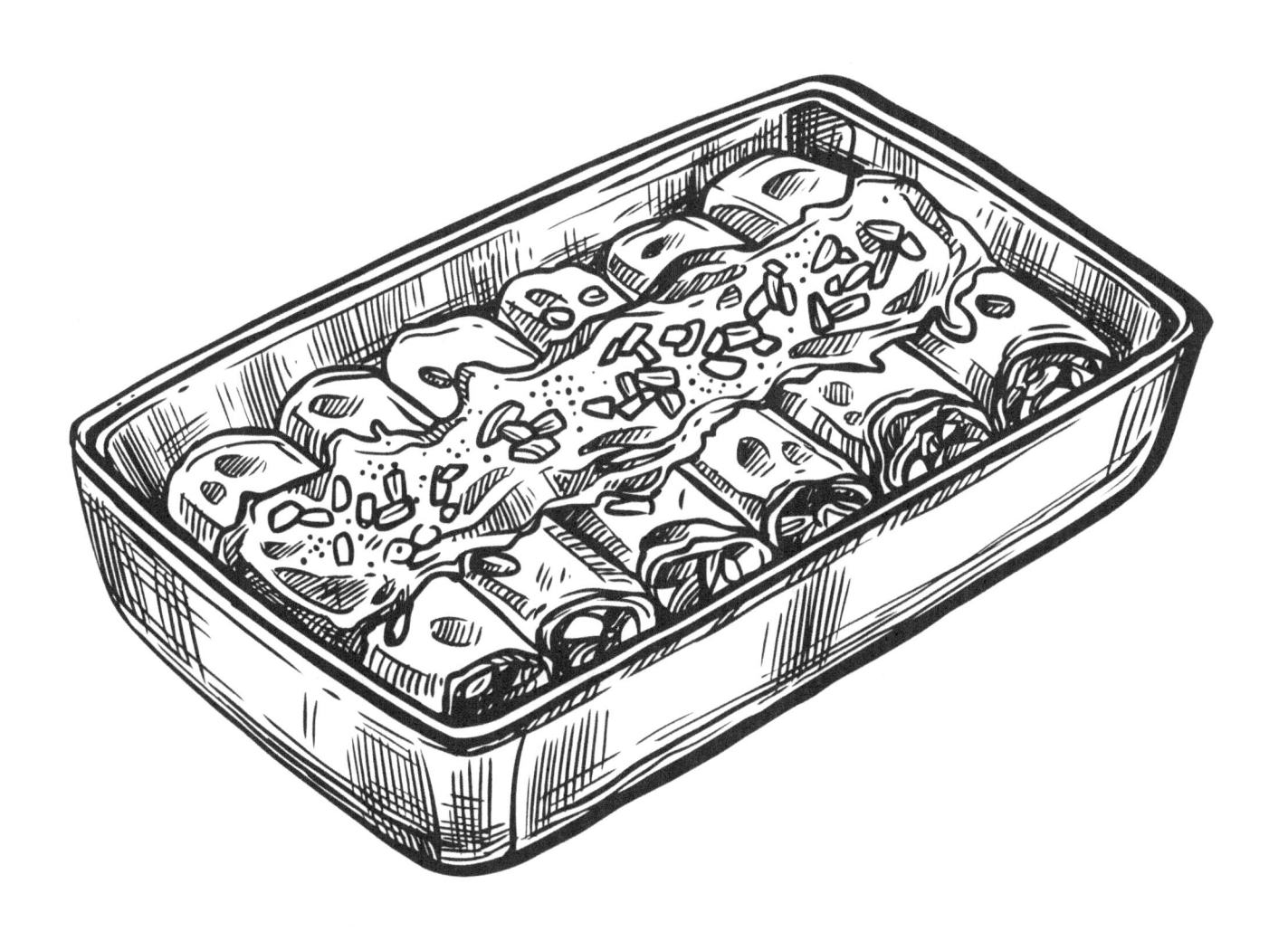

Make your favorite dinner dish and drop it off for your next door neighbor's dinner!

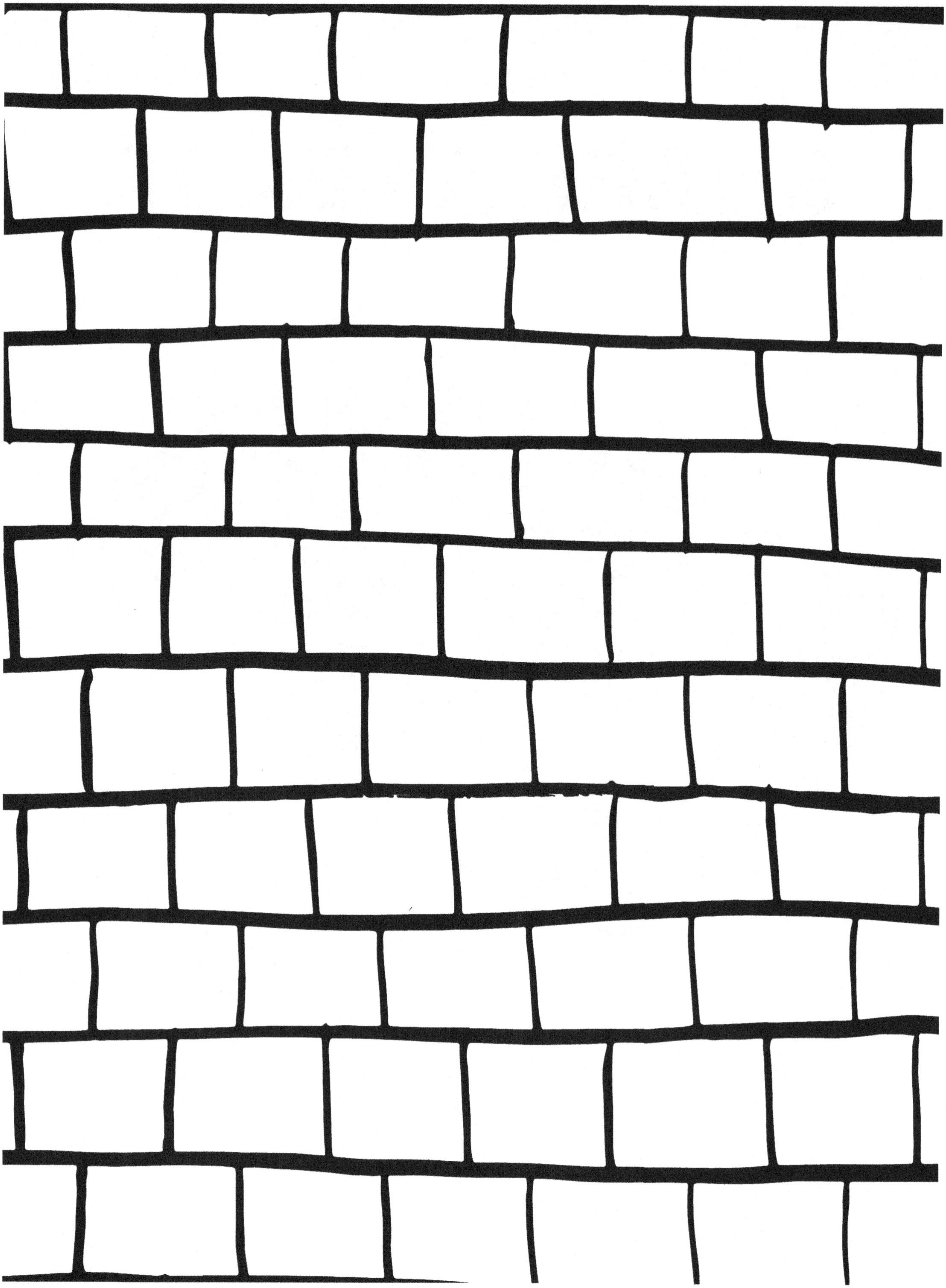

JEZEBEL

THE STORY OF JEZEBEL

When the people of Israel saw other nations being led by kings, they decided they didn't want judges anymore. They begged God to give them a king to rule them. God warned them that kings can easily become evil and would send their children to war to build empires, but the people didn't care. They wanted a king. So God granted their request.

It was after all of this happened, and several kings came and went, that a man named Ahab took the throne. He was the most evil king by far, and he took an equally evil bride. He married a woman named Jezebel from a neighboring nation.

Jezebel's father was a murderer, but she had a mean streak that put his mean streak to shame. From the very beginning of her reign as the queen, Jezebel brought idols into the capital and openly worshiped false gods. Not only that, but she hunted down and put to death the prophets of God!

There was one prophet, however, who kept escaping her clutches. His name was Elijah, and he'd had enough of her reign of terror. He boldly went to King Ahab and told him that he and his wife were wicked and that they needed to stop serving false gods. To emphasize his point, he added that there would be a drought in the land - no rain for three years!

Sure enough, the land dried up as the rain vanished. For three years, not a single drop fell.

Then Elijah returned to Ahab's court and challenged him to a duel. But unlike most duels, this would be fought between Elijah's God and Jezebel's gods. Since the challenge was issued in public, the king and queen had no choice but to accept or they would look weak.

So the prophets of Jezebel gathered on Mount Carmel; hundreds of them stood face to face with Elijah. Elijah said they were to offer a sacrifice to their gods, and he would offer one to his God. Whoever consumed the sacrifice with fire was the true God.

So Jezebel's prophets got to work and began to dance like maniacs, scream, cry, and even cut themselves, as they begged their gods to cast down fire. But nothing happened.

Elijah laughed at them and said, "Maybe he's in the bathroom! Or maybe he is traveling. Perhaps he's asleep and you have to wake him up!"

Frustrated, Jezebel's prophets eventually gave up.

Then it was Elijah's turn.

He had the altar prepared for his sacrifice and went so far as to have servants dump buckets of water all over it and create a moat around it. He looked toward heaven and said, "God of Israel, make it known to all today that you are the true God, that I am your servant, and that I am doing these things in obedience to you. Please respond to me so that the people will know that you are God and will turn their lives back to you!"

That was all it took - fire flew down from Heaven and consumed the offering, the wood, and even the stones of the altar! Everything was gone because the fire burned so hot.

When the people saw what happened, they fell to their faces in worship of the one true God. Then, under Elijah's command, they grabbed the prophets of the false gods and put them to death.

After all of this happened, the rain came back to Israel, fulfilling Elijah's prophecy.

Word of this got back to Jezebel and she was outraged! How dare this man show off and make her prophets look like fools, then kill them! So she sent a very angry message to Elijah: "I'm going to kill you, just like you killed my prophets! May the gods do to me and worse also if I don't succeed by this time tomorrow. You may be Elijah, but I am Jezebel!"

Elijah wasted no time running to the mountains where he hid. God visited him there and told him not to be afraid, because Jezebel wouldn't reign forever.

Time went on and King Ahab fought many battles for his kingdom. When returning home from one of them, he met a man named Naboth who had a beautiful vineyard. Ahab asked if he could have the land, and of course Naboth said no. It had been in Naboth's family for many years and he wasn't about to just hand it off to the king.

Ahab went home and straight to bed, refusing to eat. He was throwing a big tantrum. Jezebel went to check on him and when he told her why he was acting this way, she said, "Aren't you the king? Get out of bed, eat, and cheer up. I'll get you that vineyard!"

Jezebel slipped away to come up with a plan. She wrote letters to the leaders of Naboth's city and told them they were to frame him. First, they must call the city to a fast, claiming someone was sinning and they needed to know who. Then, they would have Naboth brought before the people and hire two evil men to accuse him of cursing God and the king. Finally, the leaders were to confirm he was guilty and sentence him to death.

Then his vineyard would be Ahab's for the taking.

Likely fearing for their own lives, the city leaders did exactly as instructed by the wicked queen and Naboth was killed. Jezebel sent word to her husband that Naboth was dead and the vineyard was now his.

While most people had no idea Jezebel was behind the murder of Naboth, God knew. And God wasn't about to put up with this horrific deed; He would not allow a queen to remain in command who would cause the people of God to sin in such a way.

So once again, He sent Elijah to confront Ahab. Elijah told Ahab that because of what he allowed to happen in his kingdom, and because he had taken possession of Naboth's vineyard, he and his wife would die and the wild dogs would clean up the mess. Once Ahab was gone, God would destroy his lineage so they could do no more evil in the land.

As surely as it was spoken, and just like the prophecy of drought and rain, God brought the words of Elijah to pass.

Ahab died fleeing from a battle and his son became king.

Just two years later, his eldest son also died fleeing from battle.

Then his last son died doing the same - fleeing from battle.

The family of evil cowards was at its end, and only Jezebel was left alive. Realizing she was no longer in power, and hearing that a new king had been crowned by Israel, Jezebel hid in a tower. Knowing her days were limited, Jezebel decked herself out in her fanciest clothes and coated her eyes with coal to make them dark. She wanted to die looking like her people, not the Israelites she ruled over.

The new king, Jehu, knew where to find her, and he rode on horseback after her. When he got to the bottom of the tower, she tauntingly called down to him, "Do you come in peace, murderer of your king?"

King Jehu didn't even bother to reply to her and instead called out to the men standing behind her. "Who among you is on my side?"

A few of the men approached the window and looked out.

King Jehu said, "Throw her down!"

And they did exactly that. They grabbed her by the arms and threw her out the window, her wicked screams filling the air one last time.

Exactly as Elijah said would happen, the wild dogs gathered to clean up the mess.

The wicked reign of Ahab and Jezebel was over.

For the full story, read 1 Kings 16, 18-19, and 21, and 2 Kings 9.

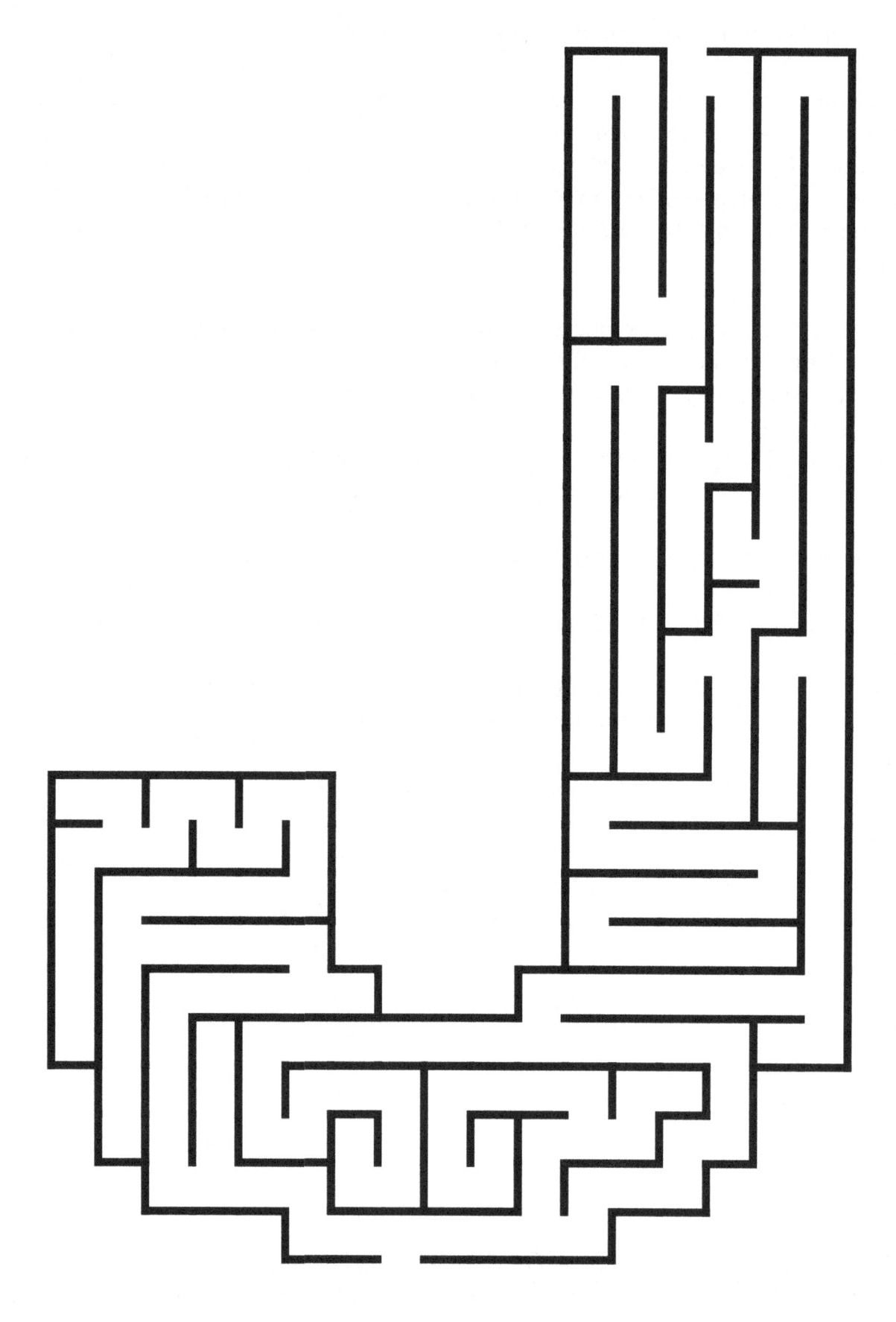

JEZEBEL

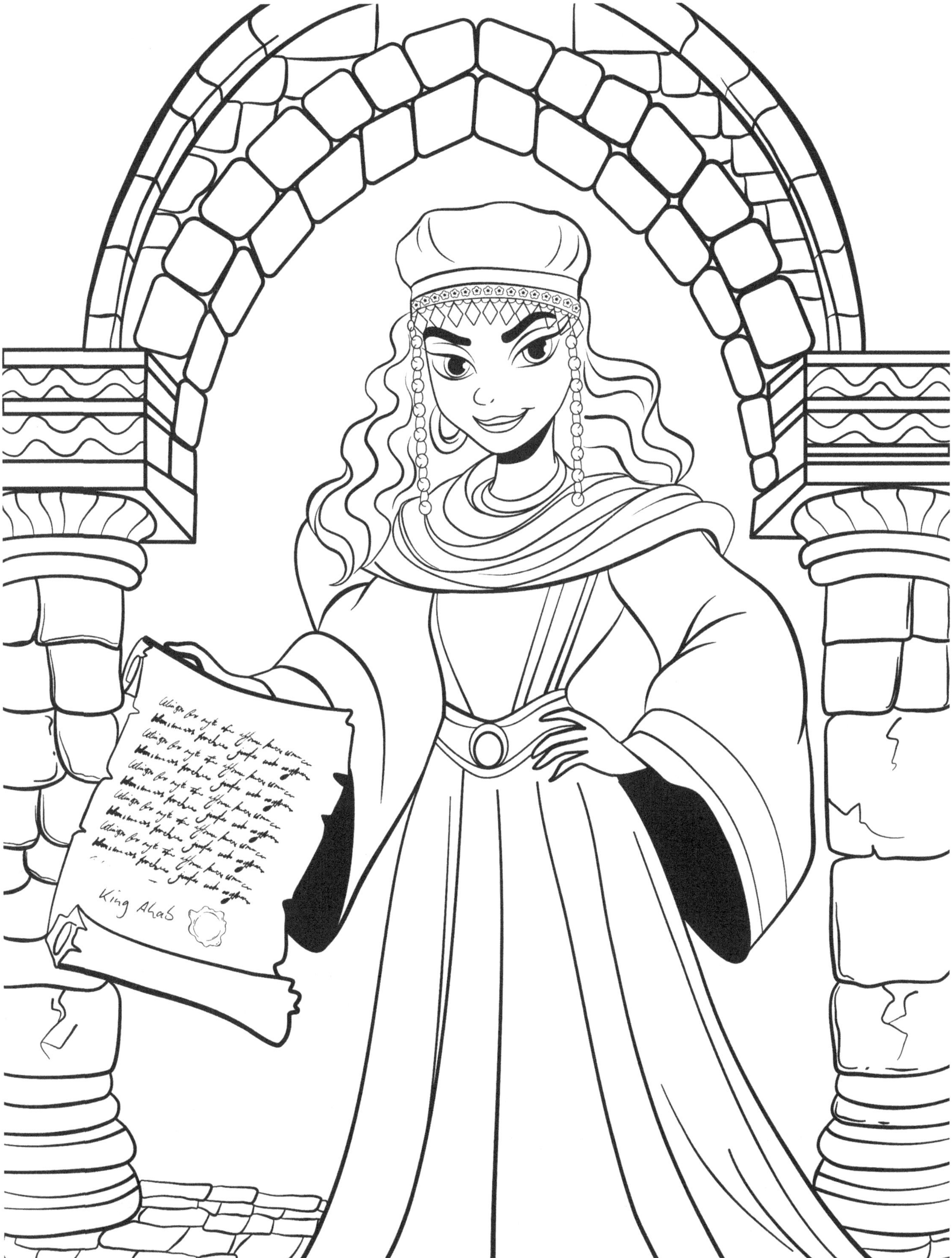
King Ahab

WORD SEARCH

```
P R I N C E S S A J M P S Q
R Y A Z Q B S H O V E D O H
O B G X P U C G I L K N A R
P F V E U E E E V I L J U S
H D H L W L F E I H I T W P
E K L D E O E Z N L A E S I
T I C E F T J Y E A A X V R
S M J K M S T B Y B B O C I
W N S C L G E E A I P O C T
I T P I K Z H K R J U W T A
D T O W E R M L D Q O E F H
W R O J I X Z A N T B V C A
I Y Q S D O G E S L A F P B
W I L D D O G S G H J S R D
```

- JEZEBEL
- TOWER
- VINEYARD
- LETTER
- NABOTH
- WICKED
- STOLE
- PROPHETS
- ELIJAH
- SHOVED
- WILD DOGS
- WINDOW
- PRINCESS
- FALSE GODS
- QUEEN
- AHAB
- SEAL
- EVIL
- SPIRIT
- COAL

I LOVE YOU

Choose someone you admire and write a heartfelt note to them. Tell them what you like about them and that you love them. The people in our lives could always use words to build them up!

ESTHER

THE STORY OF ESTHER

King Xerxes of Persia was feeling lonely and wanted a wife. His advisors told him that he should gather up all of the single women in his kingdom and bring them to the palace where he could meet them and choose one to be his bride. He liked the idea and immediately commanded that it be done.

When the soldiers gathered up the single women, they came across a girl named Hadassah. She was a Jewish orphan who lived with her cousin Mordecai, and she was absolutely gorgeous!

Before the soldiers could take her to the palace, Mordecai told Hadassah to keep her Jewish heritage a secret and to instead go by the Persian name of Esther. He wanted to protect her as the Jews were not always liked by the Persians. Hadassah obeyed and when she got to the palace, she told everyone her name was Esther.

Esther was loved by the servants. She was so kind and easygoing, which made being her friend very easy.

There were many women there to meet the king, and he could only meet one a day, so Esther waited four years. While she waited, she was pampered with oils and massages, her hair was styled in many different ways to find the perfect look, and she was taught the manners that were considered acceptable in the palace.

Mordecai faithfully came to the gate of the palace to check on her every single day. He always received a glowing report about his kind cousin. She was beautiful and healthy, but she definitely missed him.

After many, many days had passed, Esther received news that it was finally her turn to meet the king!

The days the women went to meet the king, they were allowed to pick any one item to take with them. Most women took strings of pearls, diamond rings, or gold bracelets. When the head servant asked Esther what she wanted, she humbly said, "Whatever you think is best!" Pleased with her response, he decked her out with the finest jewelry Persia had to offer and led her to the

King's chambers.

When King Xerxes looked up from his desk to see the beautiful Esther enter the room, she took his breath away. He talked to her and found out she was kind, too. He was smitten.

The king fell hard and fast for Esther and made her the queen of his kingdom!

While Esther was making herself at home in her fancy new house, Mordecai was still faithfully coming to the gates to check on her. One day, he overheard two men talking near the gate about a plot to kill the king. Mordecai wasted no time in getting word to the king, and the two plotters were captured and put to death. The king was saved!

The king had a right-hand man named Haman. Haman had been raised since birth to despise the Jews and to think of himself as better. There was a rule that if Haman entered a room, everyone in it had to bow. People were even expected to bow if Haman was just passing by them on the street!

Mordecai refused to bow. He believed that he should only bow to God, and Haman was just a man. This infuriated Haman!

In a rage, Haman decided that it was not enough to hurt Mordecai - all of the Jews needed to pay for Mordecai's behavior. So he concocted a plan. He rolled the dice to pick a date to do his evil deed, then marched into the king's office.

"King Xerxes, there are people in your kingdom who hate you and your laws," Haman said. "They even refuse to pay taxes! They must be destroyed - I'll even pay money into your treasury to get it done."

King Xerxes was stunned. He thought everyone liked him. "I don't like the sound of treason, Haman. Do what needs to be done!" He said, and handed his ring to Haman.

Haman rushed to gather the scribes. He had them write an announcement and mail it to every city and town in the kingdom. "Be ready. On the 13th day of the 12th month, we will kill all the Jews. Young and old, children and women; in one day, they will all die."

Mordecai read the announcement and cried aloud. His grief was so great, he tore his clothes and covered himself in ashes. The Jews followed his lead and there was great mourning throughout all of Persia.

A servant heard about Mordecai and told Esther that her cousin was behaving like a crazy man outside the palace. He was filthy and half-naked! So Esther sent the servant to him with fresh clothing. But Mordecai rejected the care package.

Esther sent the servant back to Mordecai, demanding to know why he would refuse her gift. The servant met with Mordecai and quickly returned to Esther to tell her the news: Haman was ordering all of Persia to kill the Jews, and Mordecai wanted her to go to the king and beg for her people to be saved.

Esther was afraid. She wanted to help, but the king had passed a law that no one could go before the king without an invitation. Anyone who went to see him uninvited would be put to death, and the king hadn't asked to see her in a month. So Esther sent the servant back to explain this to Mordecai.

Mordecai's reply was prompt: "You will not escape this decree just because you live in the palace. If you do not speak up to defend the Jews, God will deliver them some other way, but you will be punished. Who knows, but perhaps you were made the queen of this kingdom for such a time as this."

Esther knew he was right. She called all of the Jews and all of her servants to a fast for three days and three nights. She needed God to help her do this hard thing.

After the three days were up, Esther put on her fanciest clothes and made her way to the throne room. She pushed open the doors and walked in. The courtiers turned to look at her in shock. They couldn't believe she would come before the king uninvited!

Esther hurried through the room and to the foot of the throne where her husband, the king, sat. She bowed before him and waited.

The king remembered his love for his wife and held out his golden scepter. "Rise, my queen, and tell me why you've come to see me! You can have anything, even half my kingdom."

Esther was so relieved she could have fainted. The golden scepter meant she was safe; the king would not punish her for coming to see him. She looked him in the eye and said, "I'd like to invite you and Haman to a banquet that I've prepared for you."

The king laughed, completely delighted with his wife's flair for the dramatic. "Of course we'll come eat with you, dear."

A short time later, they met for dinner and the king ate his fill. He pulled Esther to his side. "Tell me now, dearest, what do you want? Even half of my kingdom will be yours if you ask it!"

Esther paused and glanced at Haman. The time wasn't right just yet. So she turned quickly back to her husband and, with a wide smile, said, "I want you and Haman to come to another banquet tomorrow night!"

The king grinned back, "Oh sweet girl, I know you have something up your sleeve. But of course we'll come back! This is fun!"

Haman gave a happy nod to Esther and went back to his meal. But he didn't stay happy. When he left the palace after the feast, he crossed paths with Mordecai in the street. As usual, Mordecai didn't bow, just walked right on by.

Haman went home and called for his wife, Zeresh. "Woman! What can I do? I'm being elevated to such heights of glory and fame, I have riches galore, but none of it means anything when I see that awful Mordecai standing at the gate and refusing to bow to me!"

Zeresh thought for a moment, then said, "Why don't you hang him? You don't need to wait to kill him. You're second in command! Just build a gallows and hang him!"

Haman smacked his leg, "You're brilliant, Zeresh! That's the obvious answer!" Then he turned and headed back out into the night to get the king's permission.

Meanwhile, King Xerxes was tucked snugly in bed, but found that he couldn't sleep. So he called for the scribes to come and read back his daily diary to him. They read about the many mundane things he did throughout the past weeks, then came to the story about Mordecai saving the king. King Xerxes stopped the scribe and said, "What did we ever do for that man after he saved my life?"

The servant looked through his stack of pages, then answered, "It appears nothing was done for him, my Lord."

King Xerxes was not happy to hear it. "Who is in the courtyard right now that I may ask for some advice?"

The servants answered, "It just so happens that Haman is here."

"Bring him in!" the king said.

When Haman came into the room, the king asked, "What is something really cool that should be done for a man that I want to honor?"

Haman automatically assumed the king must be talking about him, he was the very coolest after all. So he came up with quite the extravagant answer: "Well, my Lord, I think he should be clothed in your royal robes, have a crown put on his head, and sit astride your horse as someone leads him through the streets declaring that he is the man the king wants to honor!"

"That's perfect!" exclaimed the king. "Do all of that for Mordecai, the man who saved my life! Don't leave a single detail out that you've spoken!"

Haman's skin crawled. He couldn't believe his ears! But what could he do other than obey the direct command of the king?

So the next morning, he did as ordered and paraded Mordecai through the street. When the parade ended, he went home and commanded the gallows be built. Mordecai was to die, with or without the king's permission.

Shortly after, the servants of the king came to collect Haman and bring him to Esther's second banquet.

There, he started to relax. He was still the man in charge, after all.

But when the feasting ended, the king once again asked Esther to make her request. This time when she answered, it wasn't an invitation to another meal. Instead she said, "My king, if I have found favor in your eyes, I am asking you to save my life and the lives of my people. We've been sold to die, all of us! If we were simply to be slaves, I wouldn't even ask you to do anything for us, but I must beg that you not let us die!"

The king jumped to his feet, "Who would dare do such a thing? Who would try to kill my queen and her people?"

Esther pointed at Haman, "He would. He plots to kill me and my people, the Jews!"

The king looked at Haman, his mouth hanging open in shock. The king couldn't stand it, so he stormed outside to the gardens.

Haman saw a chance and threw himself at Esther, "Please, my queen, please spare me! The king will kill me - I didn't know you were a Jew!"

But this was worse for Haman, because just then the king came back into the room to see Haman clutching at Esther. "Would you force the queen in front of me, in my own house?" He yelled as the guards rushed to pull Haman off her.

One servant spoke up from the corner, "My Lord, you should also know that he had gallows built to hang Mordecai, the man who saved your life."

This was the final straw. The king wanted nothing more to do with Haman. "Hang him on those gallows," he commanded and turned away in disgust.

The guards did as they were told, and took Haman to die on his own gallows.

Once the evil Haman was gone, the king summoned Mordecai and made him the right-hand in Haman's stead, and gave Haman's house and land to Esther.

But though the property was great for Esther, and the promotion was great for Mordecai, it didn't clean up the mess Haman had created.

Esther pleaded with the king, tears streaming down her cheeks, "Please, my Lord, please save us!"

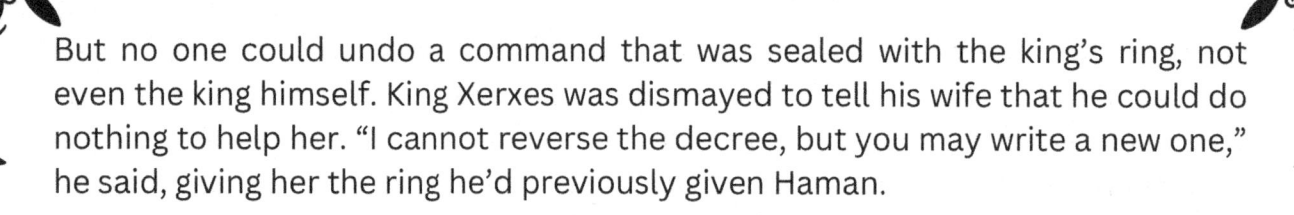

But no one could undo a command that was sealed with the king's ring, not even the king himself. King Xerxes was dismayed to tell his wife that he could do nothing to help her. "I cannot reverse the decree, but you may write a new one," he said, giving her the ring he'd previously given Haman.

Mordecai was a quick thinker and came up with an idea. Once again, the scribes were summoned to write an announcement: "When the day comes that the Jews are to be killed, the Jews are to gather themselves together to fight back and to kill anyone who attacks them."

The day came and God was with the Jews. The Persians became very afraid of the Jews and Mordecai, because they heard about what had been done to Haman for targeting them. Not many did, but those who attacked the Jews were quickly defeated. When the sun set, the Jews were declared victorious.

The Jews lived on and were blessed, all because Esther dared to go uninvited before the king, risking everything, to save her people.

For the full story, read the book of Esther.

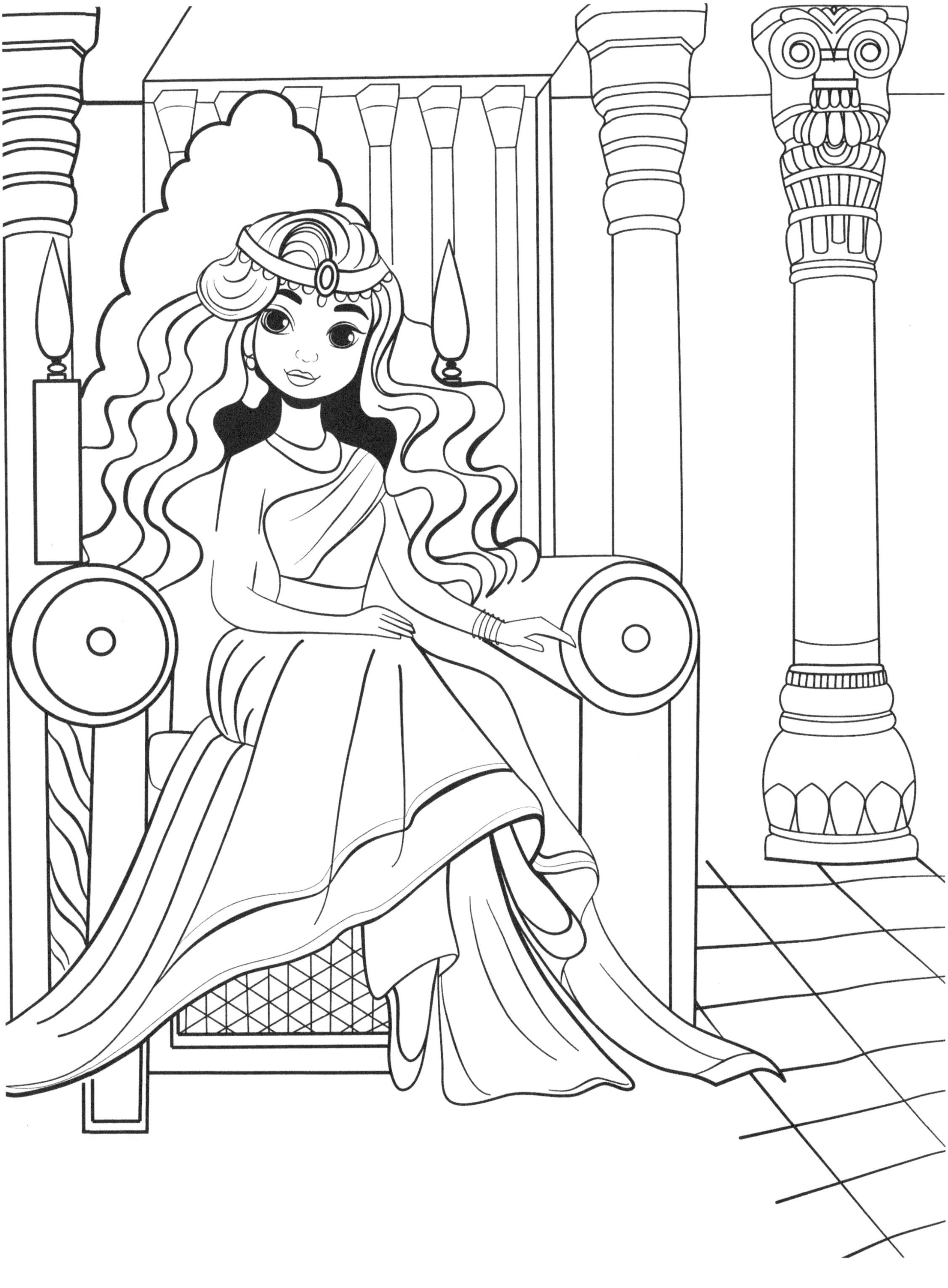

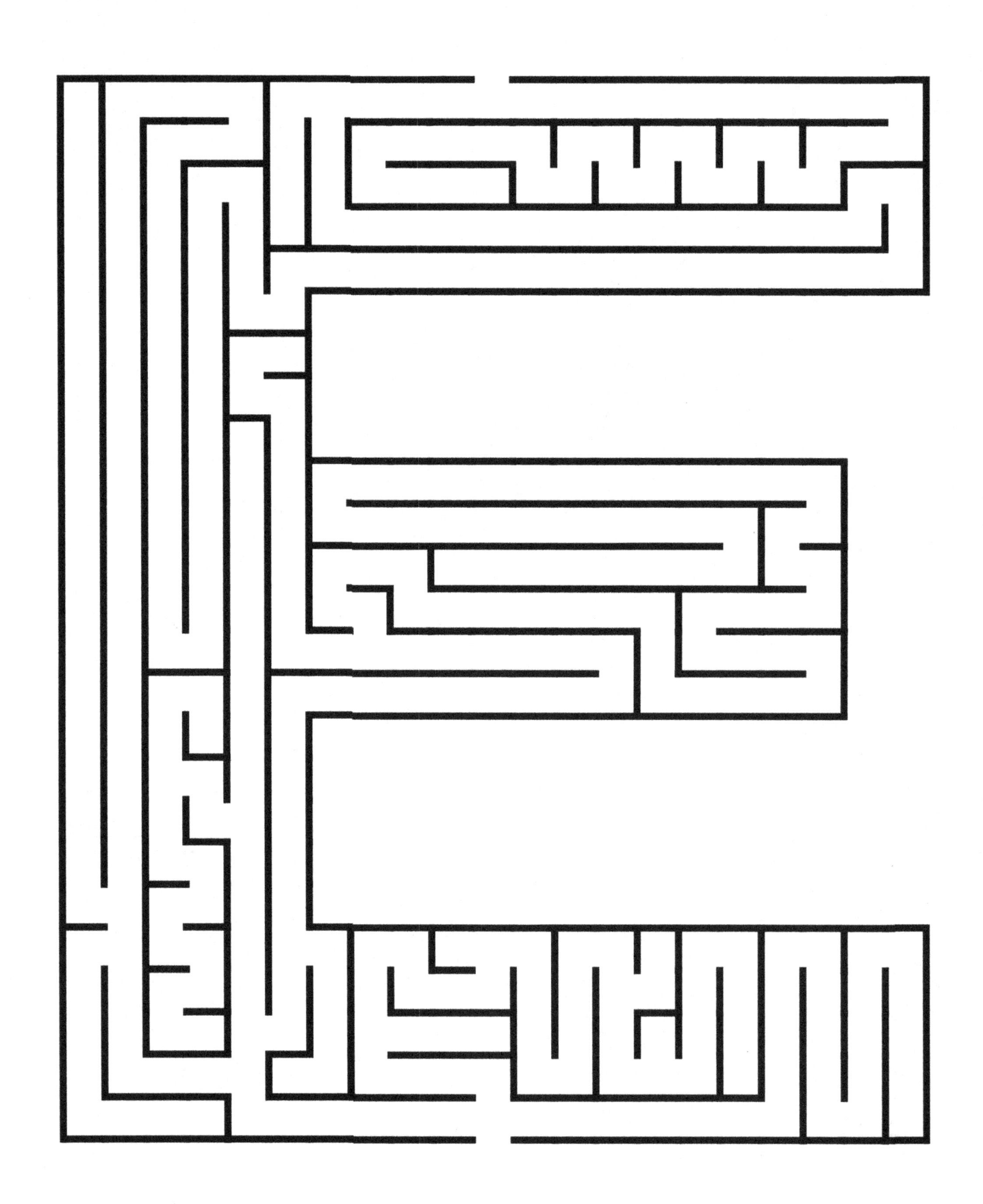

ESTHER

WORD SEARCH

```
P R T J X E R X E S B T H L
D Q H E T A M O R D E C A I
H I R W S T E E U R Q W M W
V S E O F T Q Q V S S H A S
E S E U H P H U K I N G N C
D V D K L A A E J U S T M E
N X A J W L D E R W T E N P
A L Y L X A A N O Y M U X T
H Y S W I C S B Y O I Q D E
T M I T U E S F A D R N J R
H A R V M D A W L J E A I T
G O K S U S H Y I H E B J P
I W N E T J U D I J R Q U O
R M G R N L U F I T U A E B
```

- ESTHER
- HADASSAH
- ROYAL
- QUEEN
- XERXES
- JEW
- BEAUTIFUL
- TAKEN
- PALACE
- SCEPTER
- BANQUET
- FAST
- MORDECAI
- HAMAN
- RIGHT HAND
- THREE DAYS
- LAWS
- JUST
- KING
- BOW

SUGAR SCRUB

INGREDIENTS

- Cup of Cane Sugar
- Half Cup of Avocado Oil or Melted Coconut Oil
- Two Tablespoons of Vanilla Extract

INSTRUCTIONS

- Combine all ingredients and mix well.
- Rub mixture on hands and arms for a few minutes, then rinse thoroughly and pat dry.
- Refrigerate leftovers in an airtight container for up to a month.

ANNA

THE STORY OF ANNA

When Jesus was born, his parents brought him to the temple in Jerusalem to present Him to the Lord. New parents would go to the temple to pray, give a sacrifice, and say a vow to raise their kids to know and love God.

When they arrived at the temple, they were helped by a man named Simeon who was happy to meet the baby Messiah. It was the fulfillment of a promise God had given him a long time before that day. But he wasn't the only one!

While Jesus' parents were talking to Simeon, a woman came hobbling over to them. Her name was Anna and she was very, very old. She had been a widow for eighty-four years, so she was well over one hundred years of age.

As was the normal way of life in those days, Anna had dedicated all her years as a widow to serving in the temple. She was famous for her love for God and for praying and fasting night and day - she did it around the clock!

It was that close relationship with God that turned Anna into a prophetess. God would speak to her and reveal His plans for the world before they happened. So when she saw Jesus in His mother's arms, she knew who He was!

She greeted them warmly, gushed over how cute baby Jesus was, and gave thanks to God, exclaiming that the Messiah had finally come!

When it came time for the little party to break up, Anna went boldly into the streets of Jerusalem to share the amazing news with anyone and everyone who had been waiting for the Messiah to come.

Anna was the first to share the good news message: the Messiah had arrived to redeem everyone!

For the full story, read Luke 2.

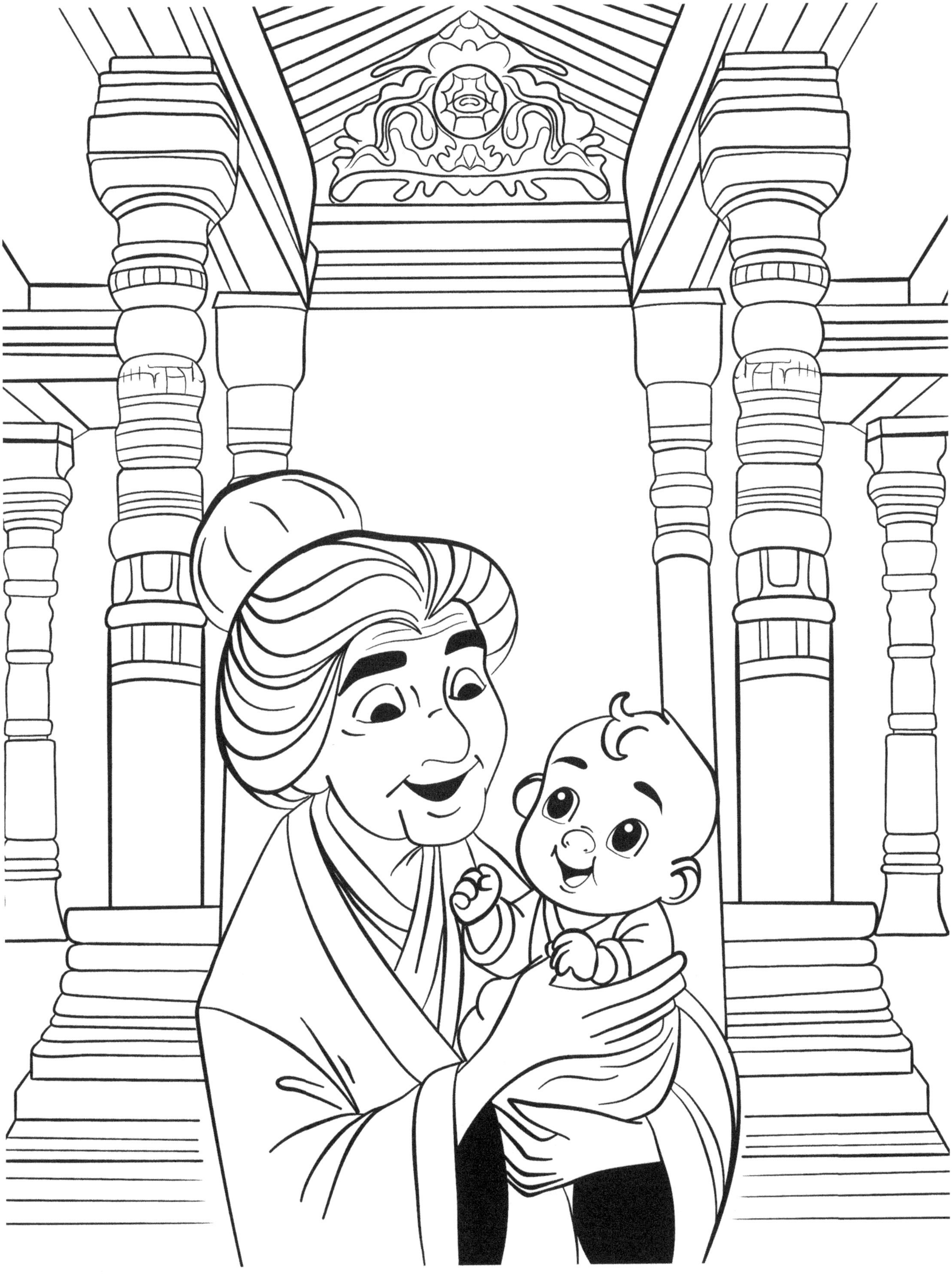

WORD SEARCH

```
T E T U M E L A S U R E J H
H V E I G H T Y F O U R E A
A S C E R E M O N Y Q L S I
N W S I M E O N K I R P U S
K C X P R O P H E T E S S S
S F L R B Y F H M O S J N E
A E D A N N A G R E D E E M
C N B Y Z B S C N A G H X B
R Y O E A L T T D E L Y I E
I F S R M W I D O W M J N G
F I P S V W N B Z K W F O C
I R T U T J G O O D N E W S
C U K R V Q U S A I R P H F
E P Q O N E H U N D R E D D
```

- THANKSGIVING
- JERUSALEM
- GOOD NEWS
- PROPHETESS
- SACRIFICE
- CEREMONY
- ONE HUNDRED
- ANNA
- REDEEM
- MESSIAH
- TEMPLE
- WIDOW
- FASTING
- PRAYER
- EIGHTY-FOUR
- BABY
- JESUS
- PURIFY
- THANK
- SIMEON
- WITNESS

ANNA

PRAYER JOURNAL

Make a prayer journal by stapling several pieces of paper together, then write a list of the people for whom you want to pray. Get specific about what you want to see God do in their lives. When He does it, be sure to go back and check it as complete!

CLAUDIA

THE STORY OF CLAUDIA

Jesus was loved by the majority of people who knew Him, but there were some who wanted Him to die. These people were the rulers of the Jews and were called Pharisees.

The Pharisees didn't like Jesus, because He wanted them to stop being cruel to the people they ruled over. He wanted them to become compassionate and kind. They weren't fans of this plan, because it meant they couldn't make the people do whatever they wanted.

They also didn't like that Jesus was not a soldier, fighting to free them from the Romans who had conquered them. He wanted the Jews to treat the Romans with kindness and focus their efforts on loving God instead of trying to free themselves.

And so, the first opportunity they got, the Pharisees arrested Jesus and delivered Him to the Romans. They said that Jesus was claiming to be God, which was illegal in their lands, and so the Romans had to kill Him.

The Romans took Jesus from the Jews and decided to hear His case. He was brought to a man named Pontius Pilate for a trial. Pilate was the Procula, or governor, of the Romans and conquered Jews in Judea. He made all of the decisions.

That night, Pilate's wife, Claudia, had a terrible nightmare. She awoke with a start, breathing shakily. In her nightmare, she'd come to the understanding that the man, Jesus, who had been given to her husband to judge, was a righteous man. She needed to warn her husband not to kill him!

The next morning, Pilate held the trial and invited the Jews to say what they thought Jesus was doing wrong. They told many lies and accused Jesus of a lot of horrible things. But Jesus was silent. He never said a single word in His defense.

This surprised Pilate - everyone spoke up in their own defense and explained their actions! But not this strange man.

While Pilate listened to the commotion, a servant gave him a note. The note was from his wife and had a very short message inside: "Have nothing to do with that righteous man. I suffered greatly because of a dream I had about Him!"

In those days, women didn't participate in governing, so Pilate was surprised to hear from her! He thought about the message she had written as he listened to the many accusations against Jesus. His wife was the only person speaking up in His defense!

It was a tradition that the Procula would release a criminal once a year. Pilate had a great idea: offer Jesus and a crazed murderer named Barabbas to the crowd. When the Jews saw how evil Barabbas was compared to Jesus, whose only crime was to claim to be God as far as Pilate could tell, surely they would save Jesus.

So he did just that. The crowd gathered in the courtyard and Pilate had his soldiers bring out the murderer Barabbas and the quiet Jesus. "Who do you want me to release for you?" He asked.

To his shock, the crowd began to chant, "Give us Barabbas! We want Barabbas!"

So Pilate asked them, "What do you want me to do with Jesus?"

The crowd shouted back, "Crucify Jesus!"

Pilate was horrified, "What evil has He done to deserve that?"

But they only screamed louder, "Crucify Him!"

Pilate had offered the people the choice and their decision was made.

So Pilate called for a servant boy to bring him a bowl of water. It was brought to him immediately and he washed his hands in the bowl, "I'm doing this to show that I am washing my hands of Jesus' blood. Do it yourselves."

The crowd said, "His blood is on us and our children!"

So Pilate had Barabbas the murderer released into the crowd and delivered Jesus up to be crucified.

The only words spoken to save Jesus were by Pilate's wife, and they went unheard.

But this was all part of the plan, for Jesus knew that His death would pay the price for all of our sins. Three days after His death, Jesus would come back to life and go up into Heaven on a cloud of glory!

And shortly after, Claudia became one of the first women to convert to Christianity and become a follower of Jesus!

For the full story, read Matthew 27.

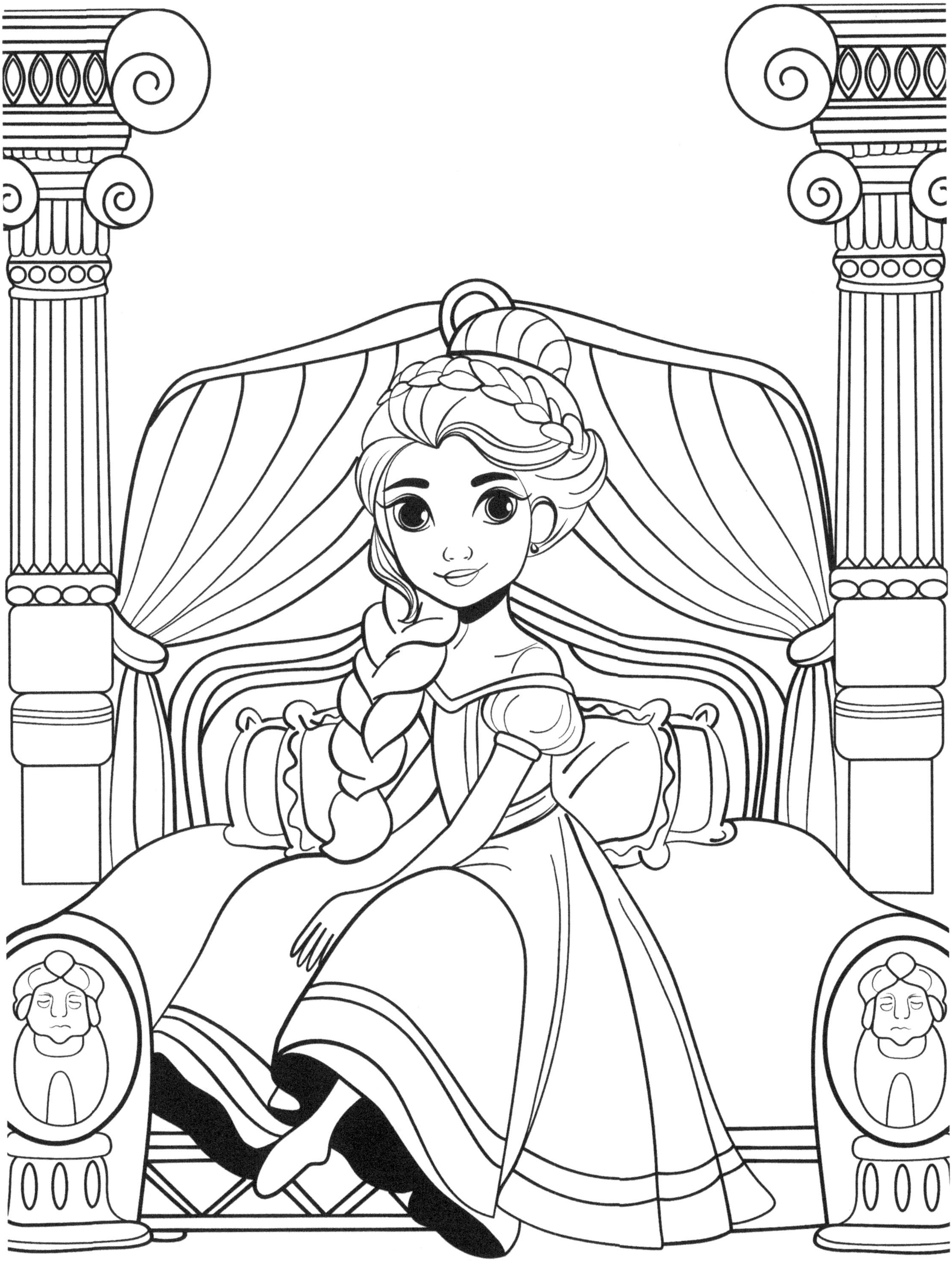

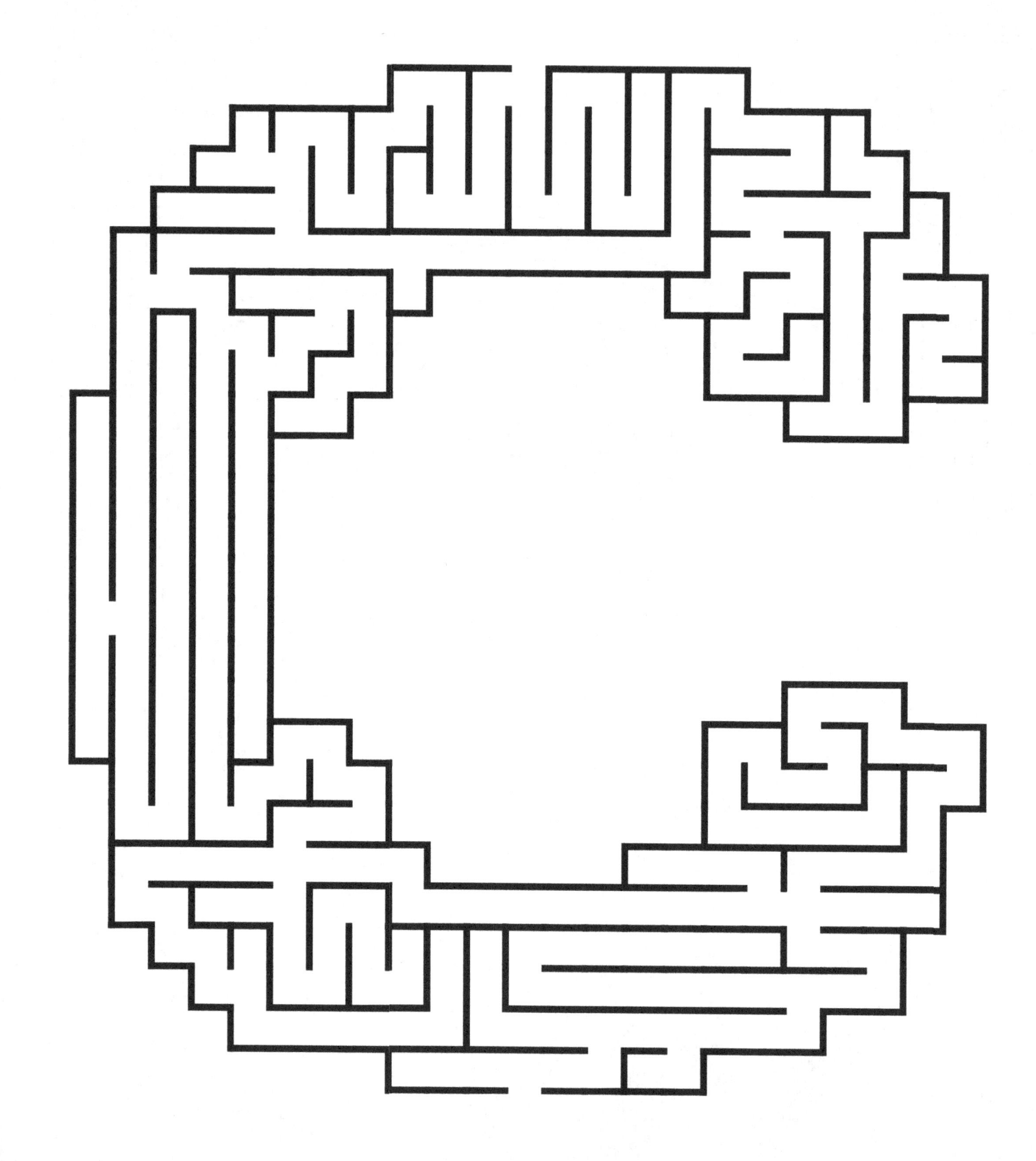

CLAUDIA

WORD SEARCH

N	A	T	G	F	H	P	O	N	T	I	U	S	C
I	E	R	O	I	G	I	L	L	E	T	T	E	R
G	Y	E	V	M	S	L	E	E	P	N	Q	S	B
H	F	V	E	R	W	A	R	N	L	M	T	O	A
T	I	N	R	Y	O	T	W	E	E	V	U	S	R
M	C	O	N	X	I	E	U	A	A	T	N	T	A
A	U	C	B	Q	A	S	J	U	D	E	A	W	B
R	R	O	M	A	N	W	O	R	R	I	E	D	B
E	C	L	A	U	D	I	A	Q	M	Z	R	W	A
T	M	E	Q	W	P	F	J	E	U	T	A	S	S
M	Q	A	B	T	J	E	S	U	S	S	A	U	N
A	W	D	N	X	Y	M	P	R	O	C	U	L	A
S	P	E	A	K	U	P	Y	B	T	R	L	C	F
Z	T	R	E	W	O	L	L	O	F	Q	M	U	R

- CLAUDIA
- JESUS
- NIGHTMARE
- WORRIED
- ROMAN
- GOVERN
- LEADER
- PONTIUS
- PROCULA
- LETTER
- CONVERT
- FOLLOWER
- SPEAK UP
- BARABBAS
- PILATES WIFE
- CRUCIFY
- WARN
- SLEEP
- PLEAD
- JUDEA

WINDOW MOSAIC

The Romans were known for their beautiful art, especially their mosaic tile work. Get crafty and create a beautiful window mosaic!

TOOLS

- Tissue paper in a variety of colors
- Scissors
- Glue sticks
- Embroidery hoop
- Yarn

INSTRUCTIONS

- Cut tissue paper up into small random shapes
- Glue edges of shapes together and allow to dry completely
- Place glued tissue paper inside embroidery hoop
- Tie yarn around the screw and hang from a window

SOLUTIONS

EVE

ASENATH

ZIPPORAH

RAHAB

DEBORAH

JAEL

DELILAH

ABIGAIL

JEZEBEL

ESTHER

ANNA

CLAUDIA

EVE

ASENATH

ZIPPORAH

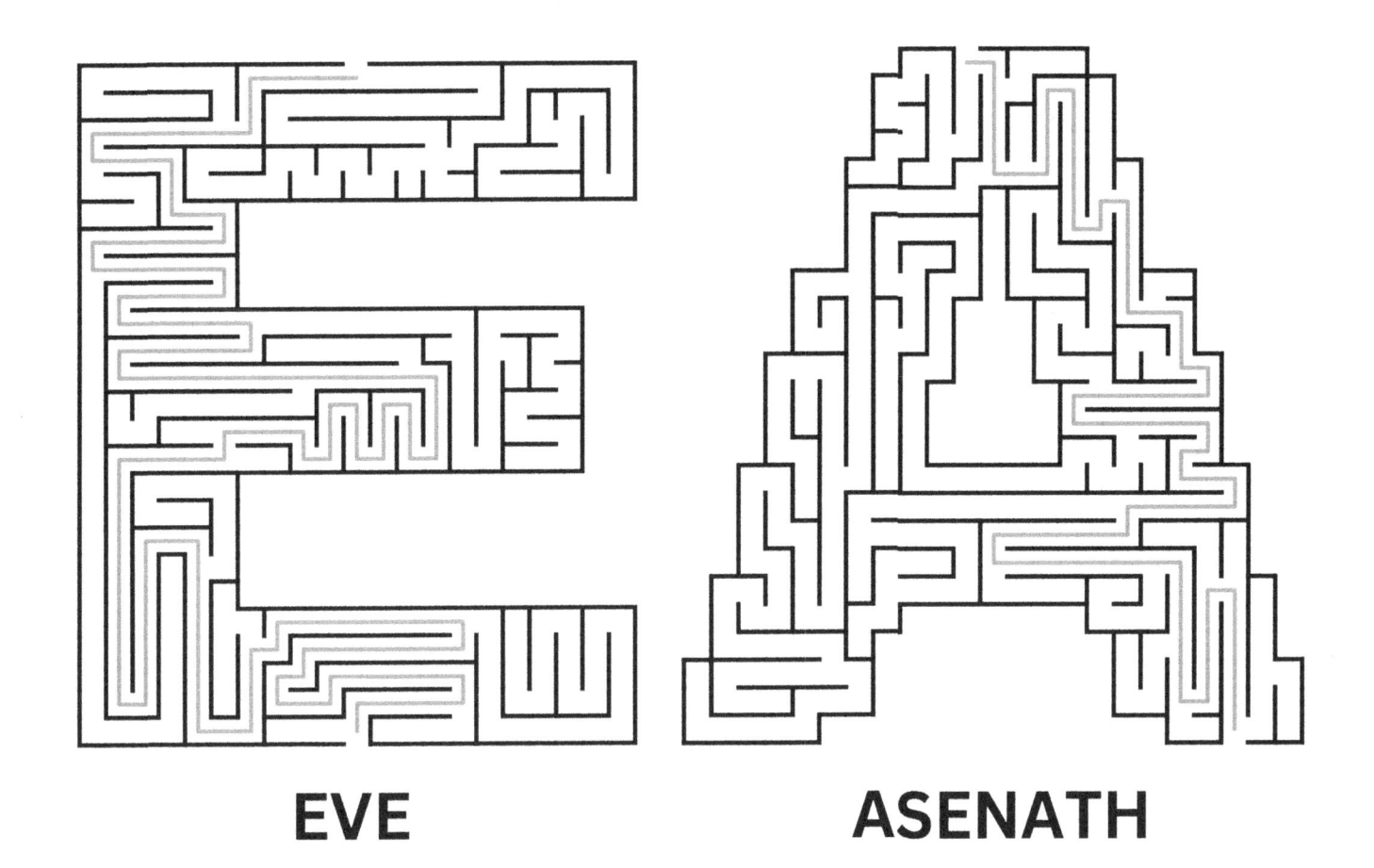

RAHAB

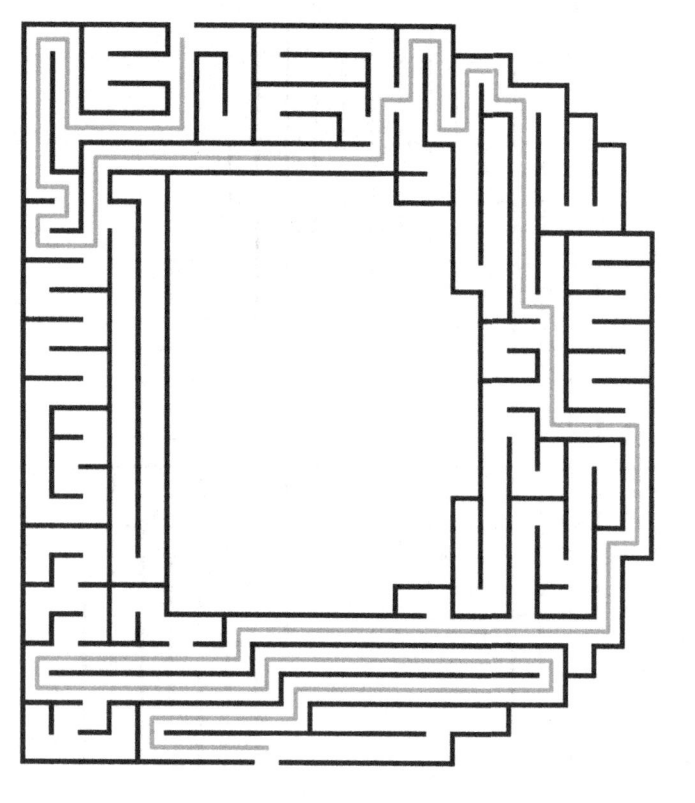

DEBORAH

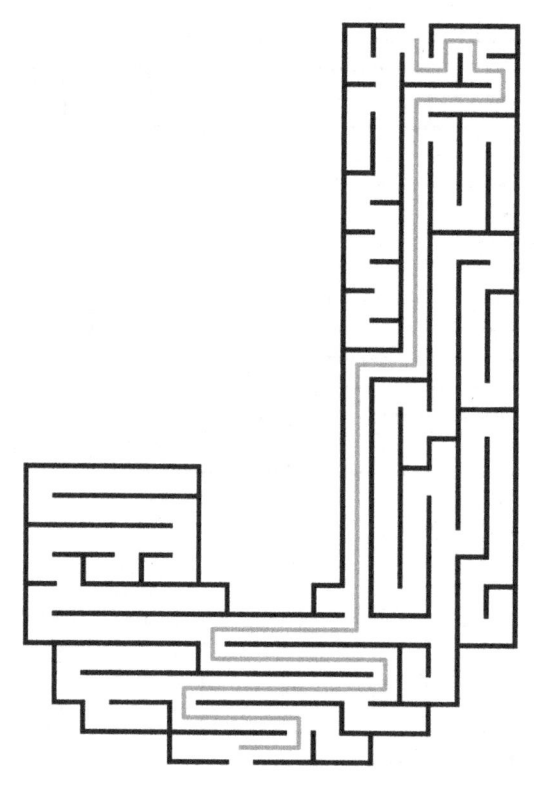

JAEL

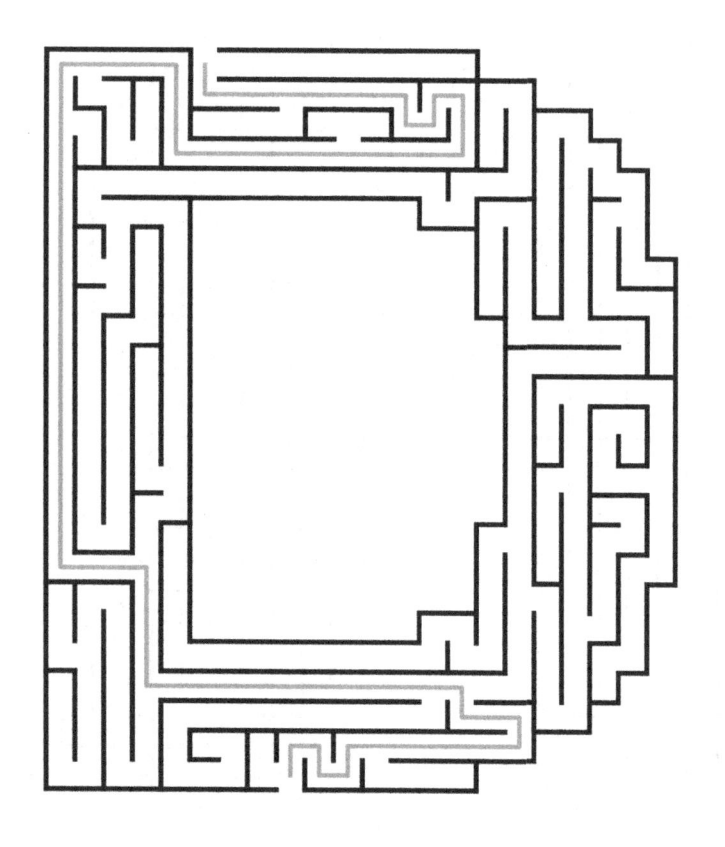

DELILAH

ABIGAIL

JEZEBEL

ESTHER

ANNA

CLAUDIA

This collection of female stories and illustrations is dedicated to my nieces, Serenity Joy, Kaelynn Grace, and Eleanor Hope.

May you ever see the faithfulness of God, as have I.

♡ Aunt Rachel

Contents Copyright © 2024 Ishah Publications, LLC.
Contents written and compiled by Rachel Lacey.

Cover art Copyright © Ishah Publications, LLC
Black & White Character Illustrations Drawn by Ilona Kovalska; available for hire at www.fiverr.com/bellecorney

All rights reserved. This book, or parts thereof, may not be reproduced in any form without permission. PDF downloads for printing and distribution are available for purchase at www.ishahpublications.com

Independently published, Version I
ISBN: 9798346052197

Ishah Publications, LLC
Making known the female stories of Scripture.
"Majestic as an army with banners" Song of Sol. 6:10
www.ishahpublications.com